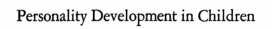

Personality Development in Children

The papers published in this book were first delivered at the University of Texas in 1958 in the Lecture Series on Personality Development in Children presented as a part of the University's Seventy-Fifth Anniversary Year Program.

Personality Development
in Children

Papers by

HAROLD E. JONES, JOHN E. ANDERSON
MILTON J. E. SENN, ROBERT R. SEARS
JOHN W. M. WHITING, AND ORVILLE G. BRIM, JR.

Edited by

Ira Iscoe and Harold W. Stevenson

UNIVERSITY OF TEXAS PRESS · AUSTIN

Contents

Introduction

DURING the last decade the expansion of interest in all aspects of child development has been encouraging. A number of highly productive and exciting research projects throughout the country testify to the vigor and enthusiasm currently promoting work in this area. Many disciplines within the behavioral sciences are making important contributions to our general understanding of children and the effect of the early years on later stages of development and adjustment. One manifestation of impressive progress now being made is the increased understanding of personality development in children. Advances in research methodology and conceptualization of the general problems involved in personality development have resulted in several highly successful programs of research in this area.

In recognition of the importance of this topic for both the disciplines involved and for the general public, the University of Texas, as part of the activities undertaken in celebration of its Seventy-Fifth Year, made available funds for a lecture series on "Personality Development in Children." An inter-departmental committee sought to bring to the campus outstanding representatives of various approaches to this subject. The lectures delivered in the fall of 1958 offered an excellent sample of current research and thinking in the area. Because of their timely significance, these lectures are presented in printed form in this volume.

In the process of preparing the lectures for publication, a few minor changes seemed desirable. These changes occurred, primarily, in the deletion of words or phrases which would remind the reader that these essays had been presented originally as lectures, and which thus might divert his attention from the material itself.

Another matter concerning the preparation of the lectures for publication has to do with annotation. Numbers supplied parenthetically in the text refer to sources listed serially in the separate bibliographies following the papers.

The committee wishes to express its gratitude to Dr. Harry Ransom, Vice-President and Provost of the Main University and to Dr. L. D. Haskew, Vice-President of the Main University and Chairman of the Seventy-Fifth Year Committee, for their generous support in the planning of the lecture series and in the publication of this volume.

As chairmen, we wish to acknowledge also the excellent cooperation of the committee members, both in the initial planning stages and in the presentation of the program, on the innumerable details associated with such a venture.

Ira Iscoe *and* Harold W. Stevenson
Chairmen, Interdepartmental Committee

June, 1960

Personality Development in Children

The Longitudinal Method in the Study of Personality

HAROLD E. JONES

INVESTIGATIONS which extend over time and involve seriatim or cumulative record-keeping for the same subjects are commonly known as "longitudinal." In procedure they may be highly specialized or may comprise, in a single design, experiments, tests, observations and ratings, interviews, and projective methods.

In some degree a longitudinal approach reflects the practical interests of parents and teachers who see children in a time perspective. But it also deals with theoretical issues and long-range predictions which cannot be directly managed in any other way. In a single laboratory investigation, subjects belong to the present, defined usually by a brief series of experimental treatments. In the home, the school, and in longitudinal research, subjects have not only a present but also a past and a future. This time extension adds significant perspectives, but it also brings so many research hazards that investigators have often been slow to commit themselves to long-term programs.

Some twenty-five years ago the writer made a survey of seven hundred titles taken in series from the *Child Development Abstracts*. Less than one per cent of these could be said to be studies of child development in a direct sense, involving observations of the same child at successive points in his developmental span.

At the present time there are many more investigations of this nature. A recent compilation (19) lists nearly three hundred longitudinal studies of personality. Many of these, however, are of quite restricted scope, and in spite of the increasing number of examples it remains true that longitudinal research represents a rather small proportion of the total effort devoted to studies of children.

The appraisal of the method, by those looking at it from a comfortable distance, is usually in favorable terms. Cole (3), for example, notes that in mental as well as in physical growth longitudinal studies give a more accurate picture of growth in general and of individual development in particular. This is because variations in growth rate may occur at different times in different individuals; group averages, from cross-sectional analysis, mask these variations and give a misleading picture of growth regularity. Kuhlen (11) lists five principal examples of longitudinal studies at Harvard, Western Reserve, the Fels Research Institute, Chicago and California, and points out ways in which this method offers a means of correcting the deficiencies of the cross-sectional approach—for example through the possibility of "studying interrelationships among various aspects of development as particular individuals mature," and of studying "with greater accuracy the kinds of conditions or circumstances that make for poorer or better adjustment as children grow older." (11, p. 19).

Aside from individual case studies, such as Shinn's *Notes on the Development of a Child* (17), the earliest project which may deserve the term "longitudinal" was the Harvard Growth Study, begun in the early 1920's and maintained for the same group of public school children from the early elementary grades through high school. It was chiefly concerned with physical and mental growth (4). A later Harvard project (15) provides a better example of a comprehensive research including personality materials as well as standard tests and physical measurements. It covered, however, only a three-year period in childhood and early adolescence.

Contemporaneous with the Harvard Growth Study was the Stanford Study of Gifted Children. Although perhaps not designed originally by Terman as a cumulative research, four successive follow-ups (20) have been conducted in the past thirty years, and a fifth is now contemplated. We must regard it as one of the most important and best-documented investigations using the longitudinal method.

A series of three growth studies begun a few years later (in 1928 and in 1931) at the University of California were the first to include comprehensive materials on personality, in a long-term program of data collection. Although conducted with different samples and somewhat different emphases, these studies have to some extent shared ideas, staff, and other facilities. At present after three decades, more than three hundred men and women are still active participants.

Other longitudinal programs in this country which have covered a considerable age-span and are still in process include those at the Fels Research Institute in Ohio; at the Child Research Council in Denver (perhaps more oriented toward medical than psychological problems); at the Institute of Child Welfare, University of Minnesota, in a current follow-up of early study samples; and at the University of Chicago, including as a recent example a seven-year study of personality and school achievement.

These and other investigations conducted in this country

present a considerable range not merely in the variables included in the research design, but also in the time-span covered. In infancy, when age changes are observable almost from day to day, the term "longitudinal" may be applied to a research which covers only a few weeks. Other studies extend over years or decades. Some provide very frequent observations, whereas others involve a long data-collection interval, as in the Kelly (10) report on tests of engaged couples who were retested sixteen to eighteen years later. Some are concerned with only a few variables, as for example the Owens (14) follow-up study of the Army Alpha scores of college students, whereas others attempt to measure a complex variety of functions, as in the Fels Institute investigations of mental development, personality, and the family environment; and the University of California growth studies which comprise several hundred variables.

We should also mention two groups of European studies, each of which has achieved an interinstitutional scope often advocated but never realized in this country. The first involves a coordinated program of psychological and physical measurements, conducted from ages six to fourteen in five cities and in one rural locality in Germany (2). Approximately five hundred children are included in each of these six samples of school children. The second group of studies, concerned up to this time with development in infancy, involves not merely a number of research centers but also a cross-national and cross-cultural aspect, with data-collection stations* in Paris, London, Zurich, Brussels, Stockholm, and other centers which are now attempting comparable programs in this country and in Africa.

This brief inventory of projects may serve to indicate the vitality and geographic scope of longitudinal research. If now

* Headquarters office: The International Children's Centre, Chateau de Longchamp, Bois de Boulogne, Paris (16e).

we wish to consider operational details, we should turn to specific problems which have been examined as one part or one strand of a growth study. Out of hundreds of such examples which might be cited, we may begin with a topic of recent controversial interest, the effect of breast feeding of infants upon later psychological development.

When breast feeding is compared with bottle feeding, it will be found that the former may have special advantages with regard to nutrients and also in relation to the normal development of the mouth structures. But these physical advantages, to the extent that they exist, have been quite overshadowed in recent years by the emphasis upon psychological aspects of breast feeding. Psychoanalytic theory has led to claims that early weaning may frustrate the child's oral drives, interfere with normal emotional development, and have unfavorable effects upon even the adult personality, as for example in producing a tendency toward gloominess—a generalized fear of unfulfillment related to infantile frustrations. This is sometimes given the diagnostic name of oral pessimism. We are told too that the early-weaned child may have a tendency to collect and hoard food or things which symbolize food, may be overcompetitive, arrogant, and aggressive, whereas a child who has had a longer period of breast feeding is more likely to develop a generous and optimistic disposition. The mechanisms producing these effects may be conceived in rather simple and schematic terms, or more subtly in terms of intervening processes, such as those growing out of child-parent interactions.

What is actually known about the psychological effects of breast feeding or of non-breast feeding? Advocates of the views described above carry a heavy responsibility. Their emphasis upon the crucial importance of various details of parental care may lead to unnecessary anxieties. The conscientious mother becomes afraid that the slightest slip on her part will have dire effects on the child's development. Any irregularity in the child's behavior, even though it may be quite temporary and may arise from other sources, leads her to feel that she is in some way to blame. Her guilt feelings do not always promote constructive policies in child-rearing.

Earlier results, with regard to this issue, are quite inconclusive. As Sears (16) and others have shown, they do not point clearly to any tendency of early weaning to produce more emotional disturbance or more nervous habits such as thumb-sucking. A common drawback in many studies in the literature is that information about infancy is obtained retrospectively. Thus if in the light of modern theory a mother begins to feel concerned about the procedures followed when her child was an infant, her recall of these procedures may be distorted by emotional involvement.

It is obvious that only in a longitudinal study is it possible to have first-hand evidence of child-rearing practices, and later first-hand evidence of personality characteristics of the child. At the Institute of Human Development we collected data on breast feeding and on problems of infancy in a representative sample of several hundred Berkeley children. Our method enumerated every third child born in Berkeley during an eighteen-month period. Child-rearing practices were recorded, during the first two years, through interviews by a public health nurse and a social worker.

These children were born in 1928 and 1929 when breast-feeding doctrines were somewhat different from current theories. There is some evidence that breast feeding is now more emphatically advocated, but perhaps less widely practiced. The most common experience involved exclusive breast feeding for four months. As might be expected, there were wide differences, from no breast feeding, to exclusive breast feeding for more than a year.

What can we say about these children in their preschool

years? Records concerning problems in the preschool period, obtained by Macfarlane (12) through interviews with mothers and later analyzed by Heinstein (5), have shown no consistent evidence in favor of breast feeding (5). Although this is contrary to what might be predicted from psychoanalytic theory, with the boys there were actually fewer oral problems among the bottle-fed. (Oral problems are defined as including problems with food, thumb-sucking, and speech problems.) Thumb-sucking also occurred less frequently among the girls who were bottle-fed. None of these differences, however, were statistically significant, and we must conclude that during the preschool years there were no recorded personality differences clearly favoring one group as compared with the other.

In later childhood, various personality measures, including data from the Rorschach and other projective techniques, were obtained up to age eighteen. Only a few significant differences could be reported. These deserve little emphasis, since in a long series of comparisons a few significant differences may be expected by chance. However, it is of interest that all of the differences that were significant were contrary to, rather than confirmatory of, psychoanalytic theory. Among both boys and girls, for example, it was found that at age eighteen those who had been bottle-fed gave somewhat less rather than greater indication of aggressiveness, as shown in a projective test. This matter is now being studied further among the same individuals at age thirty, but with no confidence that a relation will be found between adult personality traits and any single variable in child rearing.

In a related area of contemporary theory, a great deal of emphasis is placed upon early mother-child relationships— sometimes expressed in terms of the importance of TLC, or tender loving care. A warm affectionate relationship between parent and child is obviously something that we can all advocate—and its opposite, a cold, rejective attitude on the part of the parent, can hardly be regarded as helpful in normal personality development.

But this very sound principle has at times been exaggerated into something so special, and of such overpowering importance, as to give mothers undue worry about such matters. Some of the literature on mother-child separation acquires an almost mystical flavor, implying that any temporary separation may do irreparable harm to an infant's whole physical and psychological being, and to his later personality.

In the study by Heinstein referred to above, during the early development of the child, measures were obtained of various relevant characteristics of the mother (such as friendliness toward the child, affectionateness, closeness of bond). Estimates were also formed as to the nervous stability of the mother and the father, and as to the parents' agreement on discipline.

When these characteristics were considered in relation to later characteristics of the child (in a fairly representative sample of about one hundred cases), nothing of any importance was found. The health rating of the child, the total number of problems reported for the child in his preschool years, and the measures of adjustment at the age of eighteen showed no relation at all to any of the parental factors mentioned above. On specific problems in the preschool period, one relationship was significant: between marital adjustment of the parents and their agreement on discipline, and the child's tendency toward temper tantrums. But since this was not reflected in later personality measures, we may perhaps interpret the temper behavior as a social technique, adopted by the child under conditions of uncertain discipline, rather than as an indicator of basic disturbance.

Now, to be sure, we do find disturbed personalities, but where these reflect an unfavorable environment the determining factors do not usually seem to lie in any single episode, or in any single aspect of parent-child relationship, but rather in an accumulation of many unfavorable factors.

We are impressed by the adverse changes which sometimes occur in these cases. But we are also impressed by the many cases who resist adversity. As Dr. Macfarlane has said:

No one grows up to be mature who doesn't make mistakes. We muddle through, but achieve passable solutions to enough problems to give ourselves some measure of confidence. The urge for good mental health is so strong in most of us that in spite of ups and downs and periods of distress, we either work out solutions or develop enough defenses so that we not only survive but also get real satisfactions out of our lives.

The most rewarding part of a longitudinal study is to see how sturdy and tough and adaptable the human organism is and how much punishment it can absorb and utilize in the process of developing into a mature person. Unless too many cards are stacked against a growing child, that is, too many unsolvable problems and too little affection and too little possibility for working out adequate protective defenses, he somehow in time learns his way about in our complex world. In our study we have seen many persons, both children and their parents, with many cards stacked against them who should by all ordinary predictions have become delinquent or psychotic and not only didn't but rather turned into substantial, mature and zestful adults. It is from lives such as theirs that we can learn and have learned much about the factors which contribute positively to mature and effective personalities (13).

The study just cited is one in which a theory or a specific group of hypotheses is tested. Longitudinal methods are of course especially appropriate for testing psychoanalytic theory, with its emphasis upon the importance of childhood experiences. But much of current psychological theory deals only with short-time phenomena. The learning theorist who places a rat in a problem-box is interested in the immediate fate of his hypothesis, but he is not particularly concerned with the fate of the rat. Similarly, those who study children in a purely experimental setting concerned, for example, with learning, problem-solving, dependency, or aggression may have no interest in the children as persons or in their later learning abilities or aggressive tendencies.

This is quite acceptable. The experimental method may deal with a long time-span but need not necessarily do so. What may be a little surprising is the negative attitude of a few experimentalists with regard to studies which differ from their own. Some followers of Lewin, for example, have lacked tolerance for research that goes beyond the immediate situation. It is not easy to see why some experimentalists who are impressed by the importance of the psychological life-space should eagerly encapsulate themselves temporally and feel no interest in the psychological lifetime; or, if this is what they wish to do, why they seek to legislate against others who may wish to do something different. We find this proscriptive attitude also among a small number of investigators who seem to feel that, concerning present theories of learning, it is appropriate to study the immediate or short-term effects of learning, but not the long-term effects, nor the interaction of learning and maturation.

This leads to another investigation, which has in a sense graduated from a short-term experiment to a longitudinal study, concerned with patterns of emotional expression and their relation to other aspects of personality. A part of this, dealing with young children and adolescents, was published in a symposium on "Feelings and Emotions" (7). The earlier work will be reviewed briefly, and more recent findings will then be presented.

The relation between internalized emotional processes and the overt expression of the emotions has long been an intriguing problem in the dynamics of emotion. The writer first became aware of the developmental aspects of this relationship in a study of a physiological reaction among infants—the galvanic skin response or GSR. Previously it had been asserted that the GSR could not be obtained in early infancy because of functional immaturity either of neural centers or of the efferent sympathetic pathways. Unwilling to accept this negative claim, we designed experiments which showed that the response was in fact elicited in the first few weeks of life by physical stimuli of a kind which could be classified as emotionally disturbing or mildly unpleasant. However, the response was of smaller magnitude and less easy to arouse than in older children. The interpretation of this relatively high GSR threshold was sought in terms of the relation between visceral and overt response.

If these two modes of expression were related directly, that is, if emotional output were of a diffuse or generalized nature our instrumental records would show an increase in autonomic activity accompanying any increase in external signs of disturbance. This was often the case with mild responses, but at more disturbed levels an inverse relation was often observed; when a child increased his overt output in, for example, crying the autonomic activity (in terms of GSR) tended to decrease.

The inference was made that the quick transition in emotional tone, so often exhibited in young children, is an indication of the "surface" character of their emotions. The emotional response lacks verbal reinforcement and at certain levels it may also lack visceral reinforcement.

The characteristic features of infantile emotional behavior may then be related to the stage of development of those mechanisms which are concerned in determining the proportion of somatic and visceral discharge. In older children, the increase of inhibition and of apparent emotional control may not imply a diminished emotionality but merely a shift from outer to inner patterns of response (7, p. 161).

As a next step, studies were undertaken with nursery-school children and with twins of preschool age. These yielded adequately reliable measures of overt expressiveness and also of the average magnitude of the GSR in a standard stimulus series. But the correlation between these two aspects of emotional expression was very low—of the order of .2 to .3. That is to say, although stable measures were obtained, from one experiment to another in each mode of response generally one form of response could not be predicted from the other.

With some individuals, however, fairly consistent patterns could be demonstrated.

These patterns are of at least three sorts, as represented by the "externalizer," who displays a somewhat infantile pattern of marked overt but reduced or infrequent galvanic responses; the "internalizer," who reverses this relationship; and the "generalizer," who tends to respond with a total discharge both overt and internal. There was also evidence in a few cases of what might be termed a compensating or reciprocal type of response. Such individuals exhibited marked overt and marked galvanic reactions, but not on the same stimuli; their emotional expression tended to be selective, so that a heightened discharge in one direction was usually accompanied by a reduced discharge in the other (7, p. 163).

The foregoing results generated the following hypothesis: the relatively undifferentiated emotional dynamic of infancy is extroversive in nature, involving generalized movements and low thresholds for vocal expression in crying. Overt activities of this nature may have no direct adaptive significance, but may of course function as gestural and acoustic signals of some difficulty or need, and as demands for succorance. As the infant passes into early and later childhood, overt emotional expression tends to bring disapproval and punishment rather than succorance. The internal avenues of discharge are not disapproved or inhibited; to an increasing extent these hidden channels carry the efferent load of major as well as of minor emotional changes. The wider range of emotional patterns which now appears may be attributed partly to genetic factors and partly to differences in parental discipline and other conditions of the child's social environment.

Thus a developmental study has yielded at least tentative insights about the nature of emotional patterns, insights which could not as readily be inferred from formal laboratory studies at a single age level. Many investigators have had rather discouraging results with the GSR in the study of personality. This may to some extent be due to wrong expectations, based on the very successful use of the galvanometric method as a lie detector. If the GSR indicates hidden emotion, why should it not be an indicator of individual differences in emotionality? This hypothesis runs into difficulty when an overtly very disturbed subject shows a low level of GSR response. The investigator may reach the conclusion that the GSR is too fickle a form of measurement for use in the study of individual differences.

But is it possible that the theory itself is invalid? If an increase in the intensity of a stimulus leads (as it does, within certain limits) to an increase in the magnitude of the GSR, must we therefore argue that individual differences in responsiveness should be related to individual differences in general emotionality?

We may now consider some additional evidence that bears on this problem. With the assistance of N. W. Shock, a series of eleven experiments was conducted with an adolescent group, ages eleven to eighteen (6, 18).

On the basis of some ten hours of testing, extending over a six- to seven-year period, we selected the 20 per cent at each extreme in approximately a hundred cases. The two extremes are the high and low reactives on the GSR. This technique of group comparisons sometimes reveals relationships (within a normal sample) which are not as clearly to be seen in mass correlations. Although samples are small, the significance to be attached to extreme groups is greatly increased when the division is based not on measurements at a given time but on a long series. We know that our high and low reactives are so classified not through some temporary circumstance or error of measurement but because they consistently fall toward one extreme. Thus we can be confident that we are dealing with a personal characteristic in the sense of a persisting tendency rather than merely a temporary manifestation.

As among the younger children, the stimuli which elicited GSR's among adolescents were in general those which could be termed "emotionally provocative." At these ages ideational stimuli have greater experimental value than the physical stimuli (e.g., noises) which predominated in the experimental schedules for earlier ages.

The adolescents were instructed to classify a series of words and phrases in terms of emotional significance (ranging from indifference to marked emotional value). When the average ratings for these words were correlated with the average GSR's a substantial relationship was found ($r = .75$). "Indifferent" words elicited low GSR's; words with high affective indices were exceptionally effective stimuli for GSR's.

But when we considered the average GSR scores for *individuals,* we did not find that reactive subjects were highly emotional by other criteria, or that persons with weak or frequent GSR's were in general lacking in other symptoms of emotional responsiveness. In fact, the opposite was the case.

Perhaps the most striking fact about the "high reactive" group is the overt characteristic that may be termed *motor restraint.* In general, they were quiet, reserved, and deliberative. They were not markedly talkative, expressive, or attention-seeking. Their mood-levels tended to be relatively constant, a characteristic which is often regarded as accompanying an introversive personal style. This may, perhaps, indicate the sustaining influence of inner emotional responses. With a less internalized organization, we might expect wider and less controlled swings in mood level. In social characteristics the "high reactives" were generally given favorable assessments. They were judged to be calm and poised in their social relationships, good-natured, cooperative, well-controlled, and responsible.

The "low reactives," relatively unresponsive in the galvanometer records, present a very different picture in motor, emotional, and social traits. The first thing we note about them is their high degree of overt tendency. Their group average is at the 85th percentile or above in such traits as talkativeness, animation, and motor activity. Their uninhibited expressiveness was accompanied by some rather maladjustive social tendencies, such as bossiness, attention-seeking, and an irritable impulsiveness which was not always compatible with smooth social relationships. In many of the characteristics listed above, the differences between the high and low reactives were significant at the .01 level, and similar differences were found for each sex.

The foregoing results, based on observations in free social situations, are supported by sociometric evidence from reputation tests. At a somewhat deeper level, we also have estimates, made by three staff members independently, on a number of motivational bases of behavior.

The most marked motivational difference between the two groups was in the trait "drive for aggression," but significant differences were also found in the "drive to dominate," in the "drive for recognition" and in the "drive for escape"; this latter is described as a tendency to evade tensional situations, a tendency to project failures on others or on circumstances, and to escape into immediate pleasures rather than to sacrifice these for future ends. In general, it may be said that the motivational pattern of the low-reactives, as judged by observers who have studied them intimately for years, is marked by exceptionally strong strivings suggesting maladjustment. The aggressive, dominating and projective nature of these strivings, in at least half of the low-reactive cases, could not be expected to improve the social relationships upon which the maladjustment may in part be founded.

The pattern shown in the low-reactives is often somewhat inconsistent, as in the conjunction of a drive for succorance and for social ties, with a drive for aggression. The individual within a normal sample whose physiological reactions are markedly restricted in magnitude reminds one to some extent of Fenichel's concept of the "impulse neurotic," who is intolerant of tensions, who cannot postpone the attainment of goals, and who discharges tensions immediately by a generalized motor process reminiscent of mass activity in the infant.

From some theoretical standpoints, one might postulate that a frank and ready outgoing expressiveness helps to maintain good adjustment, and that the socialized inhibition of overt responses tends to develop internal emotional tension. Clinical experience yields many examples of this pattern of emotional organization. But the minor maladjustments to be found within our normal classroom sample appear much more likely to be associated with an extrovert expressive pattern, and with restricted physiological reactions as indicated by the GSR. To some, the persistence of this quasi-infantile type of emotional functioning may suggest the role of native factors in autonomic constitution; to others it will seem due primarily to factors in the life history which have retarded the normal maturing of the ego in its relationship to the total personality, or which have led to the substitution of generalized overt behavior for specific activities that have been repressed. We have little light to throw upon these various interpretations, but it is apparent that, at least within our middle-class culture, the persistence of the infantile extroversive pattern is unadaptive and is often associated with personality problems (7, pp. 166–67).

We may now inquire as to how these individuals have turned out in adult life. For this appraisal we have, at ages thirty-three to thirty-seven, a series of four interviews and a number of rating schedules. At around age thirty-eight we obtained much more adequate data based on at least ten hours of additional interviewing, and also on a series of personality tests and on projective data; results from this further study are not as yet fully analyzed.

For the present, a preliminary analysis made by Dr. Louis Stewart bears on the relation between our earlier GSR data and the present classification of subjects into three groups. These three clinical groups are the so-called "symptom-free," the "psychosomatics," and a "psychiatric" group. The symptom-free adults are the relatively well adjusted; they have few problems that can be traced to a psychological origin. The "psychiatric" group, on the other hand, give evidence of poor social adjustment, anxiety, and ego damage. The "psychosomatics" are for the most part functioning without excessive friction in their family and occupational life, but in each case with manifest functional symptoms.

We may consider the relation of these categories to adolescent GSR records in terms of a fourfold table (high and low reactives, and high and low adult-symptom level). The results show a significantly better prognosis for the high reactives as to adjustment in middle maturity.

This finding is also supported when we compare the symptom-free and psychoneurotic groups with regard to average GSR, in terms of log-conductance change for all word-association stimuli. The two groups are significantly different, at the .01 level, with higher GSR's in the symptom-free sample.

The separation is not quite as marked between the symptom-free and the psychosomatic. Here it might be predicted, in terms of some theoretical positions, that the internalizers would be generating trouble for themselves, and that this would eventually become apparent in physical disturbances leading to a psychosomatic classification. But the results are in the same direction as in the preceding comparison and do not support the prediction. In general, the high reactives (visceral responses as recorded by the galvanometer) do not become psychosomatics, at least not in their thirties.

At the present time, with the help of Dr. Jack Block, the GSR experiment is being repeated. Our purpose is to learn something about long-term consistency in emotional patterns, and also to test the prediction that trends in one variable, such as a moderately increasing GSR, will be accompanied by trends in another, such as an increased socialization and impulse control.

The possibility of examining concomitant trends, with or without a time lag in one of the variables, is one of the most useful features of a longitudinal study if the times of observation are not too widely separated. This suggests, however, a major difficulty. We do not commonly deal with two variables, but with many in interaction in a changing environment. When we become interested not merely in norms at a given age but in what L. K. Frank has described as dynamic norms —sequences of growth, fluctuations, and secular trends; developing profiles as well as lags and precocities in individual traits at a point in time—our research goals become almost alarmingly complex. The scientific worker who likes to move swiftly from one hypothesis to the next may feel frustrated in such a slow research milieu. This hazard is a serious one in longitudinal research; it suggests that we must be concerned not merely with the personalities of our subjects but also with the personality attributes needed in maintaining a long-term staff.

As a final topic in this very brief sampling of studies from the Institute of Human Development, we may consider an approach to the study of social behavior in childhood and adolescence, and social behavior and occupational status in adult life. Earlier measures were based on an extensive series of observations in free social situations and on independent ratings by several observers. An individual's reputation in his peer group was also studied at six- or twelve-month intervals through the use of sociometric tests. More recent measures obtained during the adult life of these subjects are based on codings and ratings of interview data, with care taken to prevent contamination of later assessments by earlier ones.

In a study by Ames (1) it was possible to distinguish two types of adult social activity: social participation of an informal nature, as shown by many socially oriented interests; and organized social activity, as shown by active membership in structured groups, such as the PTA and clubs or societies of various kinds. Each of these two kinds of social activity was measured with a reliability of .8 to above .9, but the correlation between the two was only .4.

The prediction might be made that popularity and social prestige, in adolescence, are indicators of smooth social functioning and good management of social relationships, and would be positively related to social measures in adult life. Among men this prediction is confirmed with regard to informal social participation. That is, the boys who were "good mixers" tended to retain this characteristic. The highly popular social figures continued as adults to excel in casual and informal activities somewhat like those of the adolescent peer culture. But whereas in adolescence the popular boys often achieve leadership or are drafted as leaders, they are not especially involved in organized groups when they become adults. In fact, adolescent leadership correlated negatively with formal group activity fifteen years later.

The senior high school which the majority of the youngsters attended (in the late 1930's) placed a high value on the goals of progressive education. Extracurricular social activity was regarded not merely as a means of social adjustment but also as a means of preparing young men for their later roles as citizens and as community leaders. From the data just presented, there is no evidence of this kind of continuity.

However, the women in this group present a very different picture, in fact a quite reversed pattern of correlation. Girls who were social successes in high school were not on the average more socially active adults in informal relationships, but were definitely more active in clubs and other structured organizations. This might imply that the determinants of sociality, as we have conceived and measured it, lie more in persisting personal traits in the case of men, and more in social class and related institutional factors in the case of women. The occupational status of their husbands appeared to be a more important factor than their parents' social status, or their own earlier social traits, in determining the overt aspects of their adult social behavior.

Some additional light can be thrown on these complex problems by considering adolescent factors related to adult occupational success. Contemporary social theory presents a rather confusing picture as to the factors which determine status in contemporary society. Lloyd Warner (21) in his Yankee City publications has emphasized the rigidities of class structure—social position maintained from one generation to the next through the family-prestige level. Differential psychologists of the Thorndike school and later may assign greater effects to the familial transmission of genetic factors.

On a related problem, conflicting judgments have been made about social fluidity—in our society is it becoming easier or more difficult to move across class lines? Answers to such questions will undoubtedly vary at different times, in different regions, and at different class levels. Acknowledging the limitations of a single public school sample, we may nevertheless find in a longitudinal study of a small but relatively homogeneous group some clues to the role of individual versus social factors in social attainment.

In general, this is a group marked by a considerable degree of upward social mobility. Although the information was drawn from an average range of neighborhoods in Oakland and from elementary schools extending from a country-club area to a less favored district on the other side of the railroad tracks, most later careers were marked by economic and status gains.

When we examine photographs of the homes they live in now, as compared with those of their childhood, about one third would be classified at the same level of housing; two thirds have definitely improved housing. Hardly any have moved downwards. They have newer homes than those occupied by their parents at similar ages, larger homes, more yard and garden space, and in general a more attractive physical environment. This is partly an outcome of the general shift to the suburbs and also of an expanding general economy.

Half of the men graduated from college, as compared with 15 per cent of their fathers. Approximately a third have entered the professions, as compared with 10 per cent of their fathers; 93 per cent are at occupational levels equal to or higher than those of their fathers; two-thirds are markedly higher, and only 7 per cent at occupational levels lower than those of their fathers.

But within this upward movement there are wide individual differences which should be examined with reference to related factors. We have considered, for example, a measure of adult "success" primarily in economic terms, and a measure of "occupational status" which takes account of the social-prestige value of an occupation and is not based on financial factors solely.

We find that the income of the parents (expressed on a

logarithmic scale) correlates significantly with the current success and occupational status of their sons, if one considers the parents' income figures before 1929. For incomes during the depression, there was no significant relation. The home and neighborhood ratings for these depression years are un-related to present residential criteria for the sons. This is a somewhat unusual finding since as a rule predictive correlations are lower over long than over short intervals. Should we infer that the socio-economic conditions of early childhood are, more than in adolescence, effective in influencing the adaptive aspects of later careers?

A different interpretation also can be proposed, namely that the early relationship is due chiefly to the intelligence factor that is expressed in the fathers' occupations and that is to some extent transmitted genetically to the sons. During the chaotic conditions of the depression the relation between ability and income became obscured.

If this second inference is correct, we might then expect that ability measures of the children would be more predictive than social-status measures of the social level to be achieved in adult life. This is indeed the case. Early abilities correlate .5 to .6 with such measures as present occupational status, and with present status as indicated by the Warner Scale.

But it is obvious that many factors additional to mental ability enter into later occupational attainment. One such factor, bearing only a zero or very low positive relation to ability scores, is physical maturing. Jones and Bayley (9), reporting on this sample, have noted that earliness of physical maturing, as measured by skeletal X-rays, is important in de-termining the social prestige of boys during adolescence. Early maturing is related to leadership and other favorably regarded social traits. We now find, in the recent study by Ames (1), that, for this same group of boys (now young men), early maturing excels any other social or biological measure we obtained during adolescence as a predictor of adult occupational status. Since early maturing and mental ability bear only a zero or very low positive relation to each other, the multiple correlation based on both of these factors accounts for a very substantial part of the variance in later occupational scores.

This fairly representative group of urban high-school graduates has in general given a good account of itself. The average trend is of course an indication of the upward mobility of American society. But the form which this takes in the individual, giving expression to his personal aptitudes and limitations, is a principal problem for life-history research.

As a final observation, it may be appropriate to repeat a statement by the author about longitudinal methods:

There are two principal tasks for the research worker in human development. One is to obtain comprehensive descriptive information about the physical, mental, emotional and social characteristics of individuals at successive ages. The second major task is to study the interactive relationships of these measures, and their relation to the physical and social environment.

Longitudinal research has many practical disadvantages, but is the only way of obtaining evidence on the variety and stability of individual patterns, and of evaluating the possible role of both intrinsic and external factors in the processes of growth and aging (8, p. 99).

Bibliography

1. Ames, R. "Physical Maturing among Boys as Related to Adult Social Behavior," *California Journal of Educational Research,* VIII (January, 1957), 69–75.

2. Coerper, C., W. Hagen, and H. Thomas (eds.). *German Post-war Children; Methods and First Results of the German Longitudinal Study of Physical and Psychological Development in School-Age Children.* Stuttgart: Thieme, 1954.

3. Cole, L. *Psychology of Adolescence,* 4th ed. New York: Rinehart & Company, Inc., 1954.

4. Dearborn, W. F., and J. W. M. Rothney. *Predicting the Child's Development.* Cambridge, Massachusetts: Sci-Art. Publishers, 1941.

5. Heinstein, M. I. "Behavorial Correlates of Breast-Bottle Regimes under Varying Parent-Infant Relationships." Unpublished doctoral dissertation, University of California, 1958.

6. Jones, H. E. "An Experimental Cabinet for Physiological Studies of Emotions," *Child Development,* VII (April, 1936), 183–88.

7. ———. "The Study of Patterns of Emotional Expression," *Feelings and Emotions,* ed. by M. Reymert, New York: McGraw-Hill Book Company, 1950, pp. 161–68.

8. ———. "Problems of Method in Longitudinal Research," *International Journal of Human Development,* I (January, 1958), 93–99.

9. Jones, M. C., and N. Bayley. "Physical Maturing among Boys as Related to Behavior," *Journal of Educational Psychology,* XLI (March, 1950), 129–48.

10. Kelly, E. L. "Consistency of the Adult Personality," *Amer-*

ican Psychologist, X (December, 1955), 659–81. (300 engaged couples retested after 16–18 years.)

11. Kuhlen, R. G. *Psychology of Adolescent Development.* New York: Harper & Brothers, 1951.

12. Macfarlane, J. W. *Studies in Child Guidance. I. Methodology of Data Collection and Organization.* Monographs of the Society for Research in Child Development, III (No. 6, Serial No. 19), 1938.

13. ———. "Research Findings from a Twenty-Year Study of Growth from Birth to Maturity." Institute of Child Welfare, University of California, 1952. (Mimeographed.)

14. Owens, W. A., Jr. "Age and Mental Abilities: A Longitudinal Study," *Genetic Psychology Monographs,* XLVIII (January, 1953), 3–54.

15. Sanford, R. N., *et al. Studies in Child Guidance. Physique, Personality and Scholarship: A Cooperative Study of School Children.* Monographs of the Society for Research in Child Development, VIII (No. 1, Serial No. 34), 1943.

16. Sears, R. R., E. E. Maccoby, and H. Levin. *Patterns of Child Rearing.* Evanston: Row, Peterson, & Company, 1957.

17. Shinn, M. W. *Notes on the Development of a Child.* Berkeley: University of California Press, I, 1893–1899.

18. Shock, N. W. "A Continuous Recorder for Obtaining Synchronous Curves of Physiological Responses to Stimuli in Human Subjects," *Child Development,* VII (April, 1936), 169–82.

19. Stone, A. A., and G. C. Onqué. *Longitudinal Studies of Child Personality.* Cambridge: Harvard University Press, 1959.

20. Terman, L. M., and M. H. Oden. *The Gifted Group at Mid-Life.* Stanford: Stanford University Press, 1959.

21. Warner, W. L., and P. S. Lunt. *The Social Life of a Modern Community.* New Haven: Yale University Press, 1941.

The Prediction of Adjustment Over Time*

JOHN E. ANDERSON

MODERN psychology has made striking advances by developing measures which assess the present status of an individual and predict in some degree his later progress. Because such devices have been found useful for predicting the way in which the person will accomplish a task or meet the requirements of a job, they are now used for selection. In some areas psychologists have been very successful in constructing

* A study of this size and length involves the thinking and the co-operation of many persons. Here I should mention Dr. Dale B. Harris, my fellow investigator, and Drs. Emmy Werner, Harry Beilin, and Richard Ledgerwood of the project staff. There are many other staff members who have cooperated in one way or another over the years. I also wish to thank the Mental Health Council of Nobles County, the school officials, the teachers, the county officials, and the people of Nobles County. More particularly I wish to thank the children and young people of the County, who by taking tests and interviews, gave us the information upon which these results are based.

We are also grateful for financial support from the University of compact instruments with high predictive value, for example, the intelligence test, which has become the model for many other metrics. In general as we look at these instruments, we find them most effective in the cognitive, skill, and knowledge areas where good criteria of performance are available against which to check predictions and to separate out the components which are most effective in order to improve the measures. In the areas of personality, adjustment, and mental health, despite marked concern for many years, psychologists have not been nearly so successful.

In terms of the present literature there are two major purposes for which the psychologist uses measurement procedures. One is assessment, or the determination of the present status of the individual with regard to any aspect of behavior. As a base he uses norms obtained on adequate samples of persons with reference to age, sex, socio-economic status, etc. Assessment has a very important function in many situations, since it involves a more precise determination within a limited time of what the person is at the moment than can be obtained by observation or interview. Thus it makes possible more accurate recommendations. Moreover, in the process of developing measures and of arriving at norms, much scientific information about behavior is gained.

Since the child is an organism with a future, a second purpose for using measurement procedures emerges. Through the use of these procedures one may predict to a degree what the child will or can be like, either as a whole or with respect to a given aspect of behavior, some years hence. With this knowledge it becomes possible to lay out an educational pro-

Minnesota, the Minnesota State Board of Health, the Minnesota Commissioner of Mental Health, and the National Institute of Mental Health. From 1953 to 1958 this study was supported by a research grant (M-690) from the National Institute of Mental Health, U.S. Public Health Service. The principal investigators are John E. Anderson and Dale B. Harris.

gram which will capitalize on the child's capacity, as in the case of gifted children; or will permit appropriate protection and care to be given as in the case of the retarded child. In either event concern is with the better utilization or care of whatever the individual possesses in the way of resources on the assumption that his resources will be present years later. When individuals are selected for expensive education, for jobs with long continuity, or for training for complex tasks, the problem of prediction over time emerges. Since Sputnik there has been much public discussion in the United States of the selective problem. Actually, however, psychologists have been concerned with selection for many years.

But another aspect of the long-time prediction problem is of significance. It originated in the medical field where "screening instruments," which sort out persons in the early stages of chronic disease, permit appropriate treatment and thus avoid later serious outcomes. This is also a protection to society since later more expensive care and many social disadvantages are avoided. Workers in the field of medicine and public health have been very successful with screening instruments for some diseases such as diabetes and tuberculosis, not so much so in others.

With the amount of mental illness and maladjustment that abounds in modern society, it is but natural that concern about the possibility of detecting individuals with potential difficulties in their early stages, in order to provide appropriate kinds of treatment and to avoid unfortunate outcomes later, has been increasing. The assumption is made that if potential behavior difficulties can be detected in younger children, preventive programs can be established and many persons saved from the consequences of mental illness, delinquency, etc., with resulting improvement in the individual and substantial gains to society. At this point society asks whether or not such instruments can be developed.

In conceiving such instruments, we think of compact devices that can be given to large numbers of persons simultaneously, or successively, at a relatively small cost in terms of time. Because of the size of the population and the advantages of substantial coverage, time is of the essence. But it is also important because society, with all its efficiency and resources, lacks the professional personnel that could give an examination to every child or person in order to sort out the small proportion of individuals who need specialized types of treatment. For example, it was once proposed that every child on entering school be given a two-hour psychological, psychiatric, and social history examination to determine his possibilities of later adjustment. A quick calculation revealed the fact that such a program for the very large numbers of children entering school in the United States each year would take the complete time of all the physicians, social workers, and psychologists in the United States, without leaving them any time for meeting the medical, surgical, and psychological needs of all the other children and adults in the population. Any screening device that is to be applied universally must be compact in terms of time and of such a nature that its administration does not require high professional skill, even though the final interpretation of results must involve professional skill.

The studies I am about to describe lie within the area of the devising and testing of instruments for the prediction of mental health over time. We undertook, first, through the use of a variety of instruments to assess the behavior of a whole population of school children and, second, to examine their adjustment some years later in the hope that measures might be discovered which, given early in life to large numbers of children, would sort out those whose tendencies toward behavior difficulties could be reduced by special treatment and care. On the problem of prediction over a long time across a population, very little concrete data are available, despite much recent concern with personality measurement. Much of the scientific literature has been collected on special classes of persons for particular and limited purposes, or on groups selected at the extremes, or on groups followed for very short periods.

The opportunity for the study came when the Mental Health Council of Nobles County asked the Institute of Child Welfare of the University of Minnesota to undertake a survey of the mental health of the children in the County. Through the cooperation of the public and parochial schools, the original survey was done in the early part of the year 1950, to be followed in later years by the various procedures described later. All the children within the County from the fourth grade through high school were examined. It should be observed here, in connection with this study site, that Nobles County is an agricultural county in southwestern Minnesota. It has rich farm land, good schools, and an alert and cooperative citizenry.

When the opportunity came to us to undertake the mental health survey, we felt that the first measures given should include a variety of inventories and tests in the personality and adjustment area to which children in groups could respond directly and from which, by various methods of analysis, items, sub-scales, or scales could be selected, in terms of their relation to later adjustment outcomes, to make up more compact and efficient instruments. We also felt that the predictive efficiency of various methods of rating children by teachers should be explored, since rating can be done rather quickly and if valid has obvious advantages as a screening method. Because many of our earlier studies in the Institute of Child Welfare had shown the significance of socio-economic or cultural status in determining behavior, we secured information on the parents and on the home background.

We then found ourselves in the midst of a major psychological problem in the selection of criteria against which to check the measures obtained in the early part of the study on children. This involved some conceptualization of the nature of adjustment and its relation to life situations. Some of the problems involved in defining and measuring within this area have been discussed by Scott in two recent reviews (13, 14).

We faced, first, a semantic problem since adjustment has two basic meanings. One of these implies a value judgment: adjustment means meeting a situation adequately. The other makes no value assumption but only denotes the fact that living organisms meet situations in some way or other. In the latter sense adjustment must be preceded by an adjective which indicates direction. It is in this sense that we use the term. We framed our project to cover the ends of a continuum from poor to good adjustment rather than directing our efforts only toward maladjustment.

Second, there is the problem of whether adjustment is entirely specific to particular situations, holds for classes of situations, or involves a commonality or general factor that extends from one situation to another. If adjustment is completely specific to the situation, the possibilities of both short- and long-time prediction by psychological measures is sharply limited. The intermediate possibility is that a person might adjust well in his vocation, poorly in his marriage, well in leisure, etc. If this view holds, measures tied to broad classes of situations might be more meaningful than a general overall measure.

Since the interview which was used in our follow-up studies was divided into nine separate areas such as school, home, leisure, work, etc., a rating could be obtained for each area. All the intercorrelations between these ratings are positive and of moderate size, indicating some interrelation between areas. Similarly, the blank filled out by the interviewee after the interview, which paralleled the interview form, results in scores by sections which are positively correlated. These results suggest the existence of some commonality and some diversity in the picture as we obtain data across the population studied. Recent work, however, by Stern, *et al.* (15), suggests that prediction can be improved within limits as one knows more about the criteria and thus limits the area for which prediction is undertaken. In the design of this study our answer was both to pool final adjustment measures and to treat them separately.

Third, in designing measures of adjustment, some consideration must go to the sources and types of information which may be secured about the relation between the person and the demands of life. The first type involves the record made by the person in school, community, and vocation. This is the "pay-off" in terms of success and can be measured by probings into the objective aspects of the individual's life. Next, there is a subjective view made up of the person's feelings about himself and his perceptions of his own relation to life. And last, there are the impressions created by the person on other people, that is, how he is perceived by others who know him and his life situation. Presumably others who know him well take account in some fashion of his traits and feelings as well as of his objective record and arrive at some sort of balance. An interview with such a person secures information in the first two areas and, if some score is obtained from it, probably balances in some degree the objective and the subjective view of the process.

In our design we definitely sought information from the three different sources and made some attempt to secure some information for each aspect of life within each source. In spite of the difficulty in defining adjustment, and in spite of the very obvious objective meaning it has in the minds of some and its subjective meaning in the minds of others, we feel that there are a series of interrelations which justify the use of the word in a general overall sense.

We are giving this area much more intensive examination in another study now nearing completion, our "Child-to-Adult Study." Here we deal with a sample of persons, averaging twenty-eight years in age, on whom we are comparing measures of personality and adjustment with measures obtained on the same persons as young children. Our measures include general adjustment as well as classes of adjustment, with information based upon objective data, subjective data, and the perception of the person by others. The final outcomes await the verdict of the computing machines. But preliminary work indicates that the subjective feelings of men about their own adjustment are very closely related to their work and vocation, while the subjective feelings of women are very closely tied in with the way in which their family life is going forward. Thus there is an interaction between category and the point of view from which adjustment is approached. No doubt the "Child-to-Adult Study" will be a subject of discussion in the future after all the results have been tabulated.

Returning, however, to the present study I find one fact which should be considered before the specific details of the project's design are discussed. We selected the inventories, tests, and ratings used for the original measurement of the children because of our belief that scores made on them would have a positive relation to later adjustment. In one sense this can be viewed as face validity, in another sense as a group of hypotheses which could be formally stated as such and which may or may not be supported by our findings. But if they are supported they may not meet, even with refinement, the requirements for the development of a good screening instrument. The requirement for screening relates not so much to statistical significance, which is a necessity, but to the much more rigorous criterion of the intensity of the relation between earlier measures and later outcomes. If screening is to be effective, the proportion of false positives and false negatives must be small, that is, relatively few errors must be made in assigning individual children to the classes of potentially maladjusted or potentially well-adjusted individuals. Since the base rates for a population such as this are not known, emphasis goes to determining relations.

But the tentative base rates, which we have estimated from an analysis of referrals within the County, are low. These rates are based on children in their teens. For outstanding performance, they are 28 per 1,000 for males, 32 per 1,000 for females. For delinquency based on the number of individuals, not on the number of offenses, they are 85 per 1,000 for boys and 15 per 1,000 for girls; for diagnosis as severely emotionally disturbed, they are 2 per 1,000 for boys and 6 per 1,000 for girls. These low figures indicate that the best prediction, knowing only that a child is from Nobles County, is adequate adjustment. But the fact that the base rates are low raises the question whether any screening device, unless it can indicate potentiality for good or poor adjustment with very great accuracy, can be justified.

DESIGN

Basically the design of this study involves examining children at one time and then following them up some years later to determine their later adjustment. Thus we compare early measures, called *predictors*, with measures of later adjustment, called *outcomes*. The design is presented in Figure 1 and serves as a general referral throughout this study. It is, however, referred to specifically here and under the heading "Prediction of Outcomes."

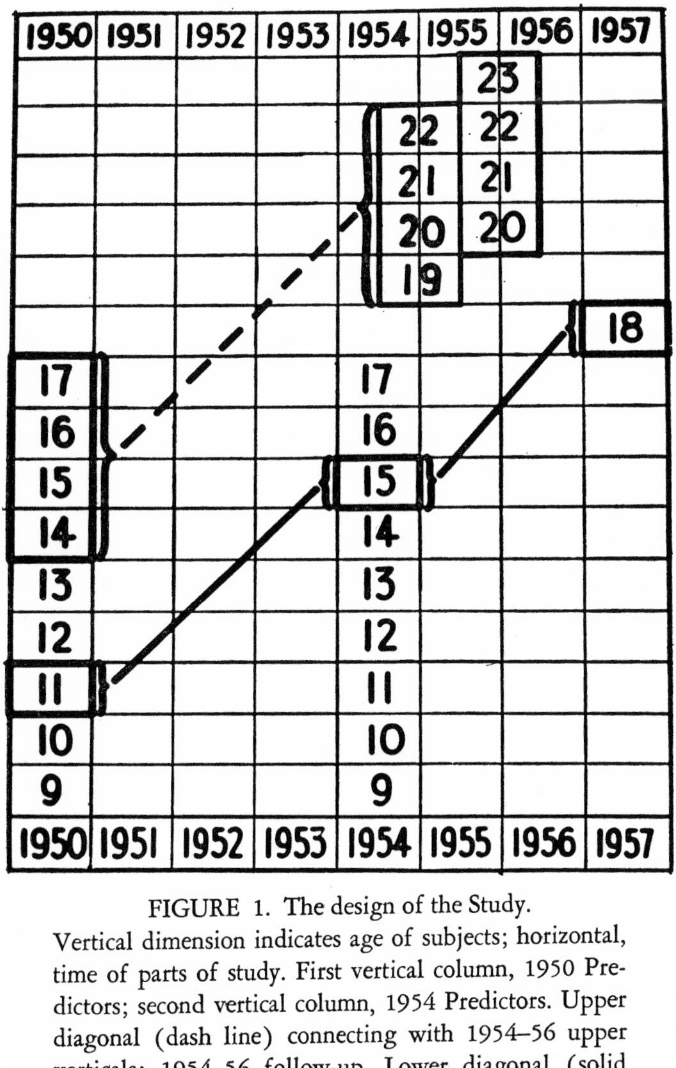

FIGURE 1. The design of the Study.

Vertical dimension indicates age of subjects; horizontal, time of parts of study. First vertical column, 1950 Predictors; second vertical column, 1954 Predictors. Upper diagonal (dash line) connecting with 1954–56 upper verticals: 1954–56 follow-up. Lower diagonal (solid line): age cohort tested in 1950, and in 1954, followed up in 1957.

In 1950, 3,200 children nine to seventeen years old were examined. This was the total school population within the County from the fourth through the twelfth grades in public and parochial schools.

In 1954–55, 3,300 children ages nine to seventeen were examined. Of these, 1,300 children, who were now four years further along in school, were re-examined and 2,000 children who had been below the fourth grade or not yet in school in 1949–50 were examined for the first time.

In 1954–55, seventy-five young men between nineteen and twenty-two years of age, now out of school, selected in equal groups of twenty-five on the basis of 1950 records as likely to show poor, average, or good adjustment, were interviewed and given inventories to evaluate their adjustment as young adults. In 1955–56 a like number of young women between twenty and twenty-three years of age, selected in a similar way on the basis of their 1950 records, were interviewed and given inventories. These follow-ups are represented in the upper diagonal on the figure.

In 1957 an age cohort (group) of children who were in the sixth grade and on the average eleven years old in 1950, and who were in the tenth grade in 1954, and who, with normal progress, would have completed high school in 1957 were followed up. Some information was obtained for each child who had been examined in 1950, whether or not he had completed high school. This age cohort is represented in the lower diagonal in the figure. Note that this design also gives us much cross-section data, since the results from the measures given in 1950 and 1954 over a wide age range are available.

Predictors (Measures of Children). In 1950 the children filled out a number of personality inventories and tests. Fourteen instruments took six hours of the child's time. There were scales measuring attitudes toward the family, toward responsibility, toward work—work concerning the child's experience in home duties and chores, toward interests and play activities, and attitudes toward names and nicknames. There was a scale made up of items that in previous studies had discriminated between delinquent and nondelinquent children, items on personal social attitudes and items of the psychoneurotic types culled from various sources. There was also an open-end sentence test, an interest test, and sociometric ratings for children in the elementary grades.

From school records we obtained the IQ's of the children. In addition to information about the education and occupation of each parent, we also had several measures of socio-economic or cultural status.

As a result of a concurrent validation against both internal and external criteria, five scores were selected from the ten instruments given the children to be combined into a pupil index.

In 1954 we had similar information about IQ, socio-economic status, and home background in somewhat more extended form. For the children we had two measures developed out of the 1950 instruments by an item-analysis of 678 items, one of which consisted of items selected to measure adjustment, and the other of which consisted of items selected to measure both adjustment and maturity. We also had a shortened open-end sentence test, a short test of the likes of children, a new measure on family relations, and a revised form of the responsibility scale. From a combination of the scores on these instruments, we developed a pupil index.

Predictors (Teachers' Ratings). Because we wished to compare the predictive efficiency of pupil measures with that of teacher ratings, five rating or observational forms were filled out by the teachers in 1950. These were: a check-list on the child's responsibility; a rating of twenty traits; a nomination form designating the best- and least-adjusted children in the

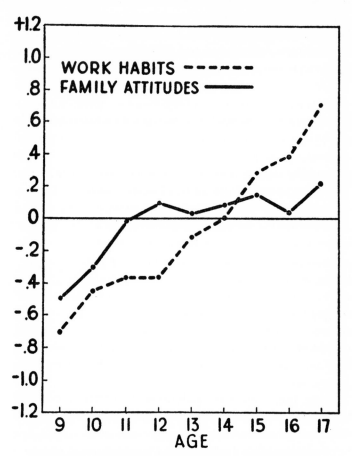

FIGURE 2. The relation of work habits and of attitudes
toward the family to age

Dash line indicates work habits; solid line, attitudes
toward the family.

classroom or home room; a behavior log of desirable and undesirable incidents; and sociometric ratings. Of these, the
scores on the first three were combined to form the 1950
Teacher Index. In 1954 we had two rating measures, a revised
rating scale on ten traits and a nomination form. Of these the
score on the rating scale became the 1954 Teacher Index.

Outcomes. In the 1955–56 follow-up we used a variety of
methods to measure later adjustment. The young adults now
out of school were interviewed by expert interviewers for
information about their adjustment in various life areas (such
as vocation, family, social, etc.), who also rated their general
adjustment level within each area as well as globally. The persons who were interviewed rated themselves in the various
areas covered by the interview and filled out a morale inventory based on the Rundquist-Sletto Scale. An estimate of the
opinion in which they were held by other persons was obtained by talking to key people in the community who had
known them in various roles. This gave information about
adjustment from four sources: (1) evaluation by a professional, (2) self-evaluation, (3) evaluation by other persons,
or community reputation, and (4) the results of the morale
inventory. The scores on these were combined into an adjustment index.

In the follow-up of the age cohort from 1950 to 1957 we
had five measures of outcome in terms of adjustment: (1) reports on community reputation, (2) ratings on adjustment
by others who knew the person, (3) school grades, (4) school
ratings, and (5) records of participation in school and community activities. A factor analysis which indicated two main
factors led us to combine the first four measures into an adjustment score and to use the participation score as an independent measure.

We also have another very important source of data on
outcomes. Information was obtained about all the children

and youth in the County who had been delinquent, that is, in contact with the courts, all who had had mental difficulty, and all who had been referred to social agencies. In addition information was obtained about all the youth who made outstanding records within the County. For the age cohort followed from 1950 to 1957 we also have a record of all the school drop-outs. This gives us a social criterion of adjustment that is independent of what our interviewers, inventories, and ratings gave us and is a check on all our results. We are amazed at the amount of data that can be secured later on many problems of social import if data on all members of a population collected systematically at an earlier period of time are available.

What should be clear is that we have been experimenting with a variety of methods of assessing adjustment and of determining the interrelations between the methods. In ancillary studies (6, 7, 8, 9) some discrepancy appeared between what psychologists consider adjustment to be and what intelligent members of the community think it to be and between conceptions of adjustment held at various socio-economic levels by the sexes, and between self and interviewers' ratings. There are also discrepancies between the school's evaluations and the community's evaluations.

AGE CHANGES

Because we examined many children over a wide range of ages with each of our predictors, we found out much about what happens to children as they grow older. Out of our many age curves, a few have been selected to illustrate principles. In the figures which follow, the ordinates are standard deviation units and the abscissas are chronological age. The center line gives the mean for the total group. The

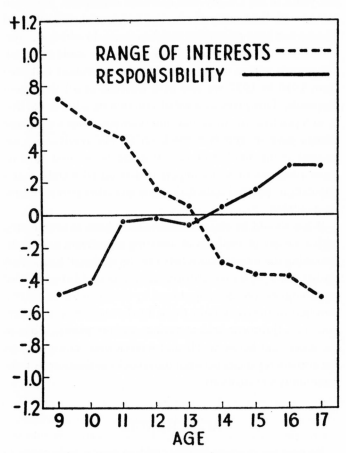

FIGURE 3. The relation of range of interests and of
responsibility to age
Dash line indicates range of interest; solid line, sense
of responsibility.

standard deviation used was that for the total age group including both sexes. It was corrected for the larger number of cases available at younger ages and was checked against the figure obtained for a stratified sample of one hundred cases drawn uniformly at each age level from the cases available. The use of the standard deviation for the entire group as a base preserves sex and age differences and makes possible the direct intercomparison of the different functions measured.

The change with age in work habits and in attitudes toward the family is shown in Figure 2. Note the dotted line moving steadily upward at about the same rate in both childhood and adolescence which shows the improvement in the child's reactions to, and attitudes toward, work in a variety of areas. Note next the solid line which shows the changes in attitudes toward the family. Finally note the substantial upward movement during the period of childhood and the small amount of change during adolescence. Yet over the whole age range, progress is significant.

In Figure 3 two relations are shown: one that increases with age and one that decreases with age. The solid line shows the change in the child's sense of responsibility, an area to which Dr. Harris has devoted particular attention (10, 11). There is early improvement with a plateau from eleven to thirteen years followed by later improvement.

The dotted line shows how the range of children's interests and activities decreases with age. This is similar to results obtained by other investigators. As the person matures there is a shift from breadth of interest to depth of interest. An older person is more deeply involved in a smaller number of activities than is a child. But revealed in our data also is an interesting relation to adjustment. If we study the relation of range of interests to adjustment measures within an age group, the relation is positive, i.e. the better-adjusted children tend to have more interests. But if we study the relation of range

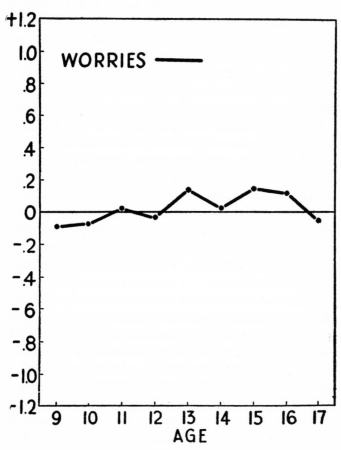

FIGURE 4. The relation of worries to age
Solid line indicates child's worries and fears about self.

of interest to adjustment over the entire age span, an opposite relation appears, namely, better-adjusted persons move into deeper interests earlier. Too broad a range later may be an indication of immaturity.

In some areas and for some measures, however, we found almost no change with age. One example is shown in Figure 4. In this figure the solid line shows the relation of the child's worries and his concerns about himself to age. The measure is a collection of items commonly called "psycho-neurotic," which are drawn from a pool of items that have been available to psychologists since Woodworth's early work (17). The relation with age is positive but statistically insignificant since the range of differences over a span of nine years is within two-tenths of a standard deviation.

A somewhat similar finding appears in Figure 5 in which we have plotted for well-adjusted, average-adjusted, and poorly-adjusted children the relation between age and their liking for and interest in experiences of many types and their favorable attitudes toward such experiences as revealed in the open-end sentence measure. Note that there is almost no relation to age within the three adjustment categories, which are, however, well separated. Children who are well adjusted seem to be interested in their experiences and to enjoy them to a high degree; children of average adjustment are less so, and children with poor adjustment are quite negative with respect to their various experiences. Or perhaps it is the other way round, children who enjoy tend to be well adjusted, whereas children who dislike tend not to be. Clearly this area needs future research. But a word of caution should be added. This figure is based upon the relation between measures of feeling and emotion as revealed in an open-end sentence test against concurrent measures of adjustment. To our surprise, however, when we related these scores to adjustment five and six years

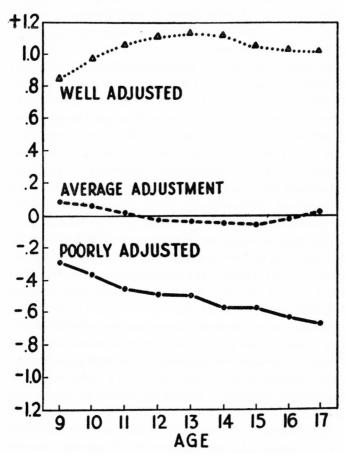

FIGURE 5. The relation of favorable attitudes to age
and adjustment

Dotted line indicates well-adjusted group; dash line,
group showing average adjustment; solid line, children
poorly adjusted.

later, the relation between the scores on the open-end sentence score and later adjustment becomes insignificant.

Age-Bound and Age-Free Phenomena. In viewing the age relations of all the measures used in the 1950 and the 1954 examinations of children, some measures consistently show increases (or decreases) with age, some show little or no change over a span of years, still others occupy an intermediate position. The first class of phenomena may be called "age-bound" or "age-specific," and the second "age-free."

From a general pool of items it is possible by item-analysis to select out items which show age relations and which can be welded together into a general measuring instrument that will show marked relations to age. But it is also possible to select items which are age-free and thus build an instrument in which little or no change with age occurs. We deliberately attempted to do this in developing two of the instruments used in 1954 by setting up a three-dimensional item-analysis, which I think has some real possibilities for future studies. We had a pool of over 678 items, each of which was evaluated in terms of its discriminative power for age, adjustment, and sex. We then went into the pool of items and selected a set of items which maximized the relation of adjustment, but minimized the relation to both age and sex; and a second series of items which maximized the relation to adjustment and age simultaneously, and minimized the relation to sex. The result is shown in Figure 6 in the dotted line for adjustment, which shows moderate change with age, and in the solid line for adjustment and maturity, which shows marked changes with age. However, our procedure did not entirely constrain the age relations in the adjustment measure. If these measures are valid, the over-all picture with respect to age relations across a normal population is one of progress toward maturity and adjustment, with at least a suggestion that in some degree maturity can be distinguished from adjustment.

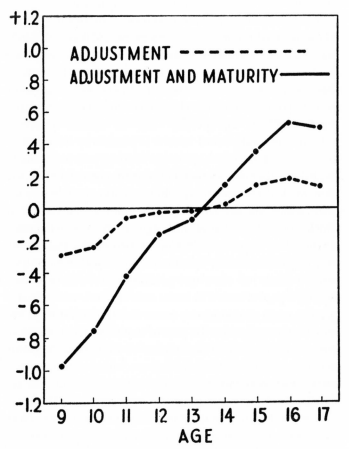

FIGURE 6. The relation of adjustment and of adjustment and maturity to age
Dash line indicates measure of adjustment; solid line,
measure of adjustment and maturity combined.

Had we so wished, we could have maximized the relation to sex and minimized the relation to adjustment and to age (or maturity), and thus secured marked sex differences. Other combinations are possible. In maximizing, a fiducial limit in terms of a high significance figure was set for items to be retained; and in minimizing, a low fiducial limit was set for the item. Then these limits must be applied simultaneously for each criterion used to each of the items in the pool.

In these figures sex differences are not shown. In fact, age-sex difference plots, based on our 1950 and our 1954 measures, generally show insignificant differences with respect to sex. So much is this true that in the early years of this study, when we were concerned with the predictors, we felt that we could ignore sex differences even though they appeared as a matter of routine in the statistical analysis. In terms of concurrent validation, clear relations to sex do not emerge. However, when we moved into the study of outcomes and the long-time view of adjustment, sex differences became important; thus we went back and reanalyzed some of our data with the result that relatively low overlap was found in the items which predicted adjustment for girls over a long time, when compared with those that predicted for boys. This is an area that needs further examination with extensive item-analysis and examination of item content in terms of its relevance both to sex and to later adjustment.

In our age-relation data there is evidence among various measures of differential changes with age. In some there is a fairly uniform increase throughout the whole of development; in some the increases seem to come mainly prior to puberty; and in some, they come mainly in the adolescent years. This may be an effect of the ceilings and floors of the particular measuring instrument and of the units of measurement used. But since we reduced all measures to a common base in terms of standard scores, we corrected, in some degree, for the differences in scales and units. Since such differential change with age is commonly found for many measures in the area of physical growth, it is not unreasonable to expect the principle to hold for mental growth.

In all areas in which we deal with the competence of the individual as measured by skill, knowledge, problem-solving, interest, work habits, etc., there seem to be consistent changes with age; whereas in the measures which deal with feelings and emotions, little evidence of change with age appears. Some of the attitude measures which change moderately with age occupy an intermediate position.

The discovery of measures in which there are no age changes was unexpected and has led to some speculation. It may well be that age changes in emotional and feeling areas are present at early ages and that responses were stabilized by the time we studied these children. Since the earliest age we studied was nine years, we dealt with children well along in their developmental course. This suggests studies at earlier age levels. Nevertheless, the concept of age-bound and age-free phenomena in development seems worth exploring at all age levels.

THE PREDICTION OF OUTCOMES

In the following sections various types of results will be presented. We have so much data and so many predictors and outcomes that we could spend hours on detail. It is clear from the mass of data that there is no simple and pat answer to the scientific and practical problems we faced and that by presenting too many details we raise more questions than we can answer. For our present purpose, then, we will first give general findings for the prediction of the psychological assessment of selected persons in the 1955–56 follow-up, represented by the top diagonal in Figure 1. Next come the predictions of the assessments made in school and community for the cohort of persons who were first examined as eleven year olds in 1950, at fifteen years in 1954, and followed up at eighteen years in 1957. This group is represented in the lower diagonal of Figure 1. These figures are presented in the form of correlation coefficients with the level of significance indicated.

Next, we will present data which are concerned with the outcomes in terms of the criteria for social adjustment as shown in the records of the outstanding persons, those who dropped out of school, and those who were delinquent or emotionally disturbed. For this data comparisons are made with the means for the entire sample in terms of significance at the 5-per-cent level. Finally, we will present the results of an attempt at cross-validation by checking the predictive power of the 1957 follow-up of items selected from the 1955–56 follow-up.

In interpreting the correlations obtained, some consideration must go to the size of the coefficient that can be expected when a phenomenon at one age level in a growing organism is correlated with the same phenomenon some years later. Not many data are available on this problem, since the answer depends upon longitudinal data from the same individuals at successive ages. I made a study (1) based on the Harvard growth data. Going from intelligence quotients at a mean age of 10.43 years for boys to those for the same boys at 16.42 years, an r of $+.74$ was obtained; whereas for girls, going from a mean of 10.40 years to a mean of 16.39 years the r was $+.70$. This is a span of six years. Bayley (4), going from Stanford-Binets at eleven years to Wechsler-Bellevues at eighteen years, obtained an r of $+.93$ for boys and girls combined, a span of seven years. Tuddenham and Snyder (16) correlated various physical measures. For height there was an r of .88 for boys between eleven and eighteen years, and an r of .73 between girls at eleven years and eighteen years. For a series of five other physical measurements, the r's over the seven year span range from .73 to .88 for boys and from .71 to .79 for girls. For strength they found *r*'s of +.72 for boys and of +.70 for girls. I have selected these spans as near in length to the span covered in the Nobles County study. The essential point is that in evaluating the relations of measures of adjustment over a substantial period of time, we literally do not know what the relation would be if a perfect measure of adjustment could be obtained at eleven years and another perfect measure at eighteen years. Some change that affects the size of the coefficient certainly occurs. Moreover, from the figures presented for the above reliable and well-validated measures, it is clear that the relation would not be 100 but well under that figure. For measures separated by long periods of time, intercorrelations decrease with the length of the interval. This drop is much greater during a period in which growth is rapid than during one in which the organism is at a maintenance level.

Predictors in 1950 vs. 1955–56 Assessment. For both boys and girls Table 1 presents the correlations between classes of measures from the 1950 data and various aspects of the 1955–56 assessment of adjustment. These include the intelligence quotient, a measure of socio-economic status, the pupil index which is a combination of the personality measures and the teacher index, a combination of the teachers' ratings. For the boys it is a five-year follow-up and for the girls a six-year follow-up, with the mean ages of both sexes at the time of original measurement being sixteen and at the time of the final measurement twenty-one for the boys and twenty-two for the girls. With but one exception (the correlation between teacher index and self-rating for the boys, which is −.18), all the coefficients are positive. Eighteen of the forty are above the 1-per-cent level of significance and an additional six above the 5-per-cent level. For the boys, IQ, socio-economic status, and pupil index predict the total combined adjustment index,

TABLE 1. 1950 Predictors *vs.* 1955–56 Follow-Up

	BOYS (n = 76)				
1950	Adjust-ment Index	Inter-view	Self-Rating	Morale	Repu-tation
1950 IQ	.32**	.39**	.08	.18	.29**
Socio-Economic Status	.25*	.26*	.14	.11	.23*
Pupil Index	.29**	.35**	.02	.15	.29**
Teacher Index	.11	.18	—.18	.05	.41**

	GIRLS (n = 79)				
1950	Adjust-ment Index	Inter-view	Self-Rating	Morale	Repu-tation
1950 IQ	.21	.06	.12	.22*	.20
Socio-Economic Status	.31**	.31**	.22*	.30**	.13
Pupil Index	.52**	.36**	.60**	.48**	.17
Teacher Index	.48**	.37**	.52**	.25*	.37**

* 5% level *r* = .22 up
** 1% level *r* = .29 up

but the teacher index does not. They also predict the self-ratings or the score on the morale inventory. Note the good relation of the teacher index to the community-reputation score, which suggests some commonality in the way boys appear to teachers earlier and to community informants later.

For the girls the correlations with final outcomes are in general lower with IQ, higher with socio-economic status, and much higher with both the pupil index and the teacher index. Particularly to be noticed is the fact that the teacher index predicts the outcome for the girls in all aspects of adjustment much more satisfactorily than it does for the boys. Note also the very high correlations of both the pupil index and the teacher index with the girls' ratings of themselves as contrasted with the negative or slight relationship that holds for the boys.

The striking feature of this table is the quite different pattern of correlation coefficients obtained for boys and for girls and the obvious differential prediction of the various aspects of the follow-up. In considering these results it should be noted that we used a male to interview the boys and a female for the girls. This offers a possible explanation of these differences. However, the interviewers were both trained psychologists who spent much time in trying to equate their interviewing procedures and who used similar schedules in obtaining their data. But there also is the possibility that this difference may represent a real difference in the adjustment pattern of the girl and the boy in the period from nineteen to twenty-three years, account of which must be taken for predicting later adjustment. There is also a suggestion, when we look at the results of the teacher index for both sexes, that teachers are better able to predict outcomes for their own than for the opposite sex.

Predictions from 1950 to the 1957 Follow-Up. For the cohort that was followed through from eleven to eighteen years of age, Table 2 gives the correlation coefficients for IQ, the pupil index, the teacher index and a combination of the three with the outcomes as represented by a combined score, together with the components of that score, a school score, and an informant's score, along with the participation score which is independent of the combined score. The coefficients in this table are all positive and of the thirty-two obtained, twenty-two are significant above the 1-per-cent level and five more above the 5-per-cent level. For both boys and girls IQ is a very substantial predictor of adjustment outcomes; the pupil index is less effective for boys and quite ineffective for the girls; and the teacher index is an effective predictor for both boys and girls. Although the combination of IQ, the pupil index, and the teacher index gives good predictions, the results are consistently better for the boys than the girls. At some points the coefficients drop. The pupil index for the boys

TABLE 2. 1950 Predictors *vs.* 1957 Cohort Follow-Up

BOYS ($n = 74$)				
1950	Combina-tion Score	School Score	Inform-ants' Score	Partic-ipation
IQ	.52**	.58**	.37**	.56**
Pupil Index	.29**	.28*	.23*	.17
Teacher Index	.53**	.56**	.40**	.40**
IQ + PI + TI	.62**	.66**	.46**	.55**

GIRLS ($n = 65$)				
1950	Combina-tion Score	School Score	Inform-ants' Score	Partic-ipation
IQ	.45**	.56**	.27*	.43**
Pupil Index	.04	.12	.17	.26*
Teacher Index	.54**	.52**	.44**	.17
IQ + PI + TI	.48**	.60**	.24*	.38**

* 5% level $r = .22$ up
** 1% level $r = .29$ up

does not predict participation and for the girls the pupil index does not predict the combination score or its various parts, although it predicts participation. The teacher index does not predict participation for the girls.

One of the problems raised by the results of Table 2, when compared with those of Table 1, centers in contradiction in the findings with respect to sex differences. Although the coefficients in Table 2 are in general lower for the girls than for the boys, there is little evidence of the difference in pattern which appeared in Table 1. We must remember that the measures of adjustment are quite different, since those used in 1957 are much more closely tied to the school situation. This is probably true for the information given about the person by informants, even though we did not use school people as informants in order to minimize halo effects. In the 1957 follow-up, IQ holds up for both sexes, whereas in 1955–56 it held up for the boys, not the girls; the pupil index in 1957 holds up for the boys, but not for the girls, whereas in 1955–56 it held up for both sexes but especially for the girls. The teacher index in 1957 holds up for both sexes, while in 1955–56 it held up for the girls and not for the boys. While I suspect that these differences may be mainly in the criteria for adjustment, some consideration should also go to the situation the girl and boy face in adjustment at the age of eighteen years when the 1957 follow-up was done, as compared with the situation that is faced at twenty-one or twenty-two years when the 1955–56 follow-up was done. For Table 2 we have persons who have made their record in school and are just out. For Table 1, however, the persons studied are mainly in the early years of marriage.

Nevertheless, we feel that the problem of sex differences in adjustment deserves serious consideration. When we started this project and used concurrent validation on our instruments, the sex differences obtained were relatively slight. In the age curves presented earlier, I combined the sexes because we found only slight age-sex trends. Yet the analysis of the relation of our predictor data to our outcomes data suggests differences.

In a later part of our study, we tried by an item-analysis to select from our whole pool of 1950 measures the particular items which predicted the adjustment of the girls and those which predicted the adjustment of the boys five and six years later. When these items were examined in the terms of their discriminative value, there appeared only a 10-per-cent overlap among the items, that is, only 10 per cent of the very highly discriminative items were common to both scales. This is a surprisingly small overlap in terms of what we had expected on the basis of our earlier studies of these instruments on a cross-section or concurrent validation basis.

Predictors and Social Criteria. In Table 3 the relation of predictors to our various social criteria is presented. The outstanding children and youth in the various communities in the

TABLE 3. Predictors *vs.* Social Criteria

BOYS	Out-standing	Drop-Outs	Delin-quents	Emotionally Disturbed
1950 IQ	+	−	0	*
Socio-Economic Status	+	−	−	*
Pupil Index 1950	+	0	0	*
Pupil Index 1954	+	−	−	*
Teacher Index 1950	+	−	−	*

GIRLS	Out-standing	Drop-Outs	Delin-quents	Emotionally Disturbed
1950 IQ	+	−	0	+
Socio-Economic Status	+	−	0	0
Pupil Index 1950	+	0	0	0
Pupil Index 1954	+	−	0	0
Teacher Index 1950	+	−	0	0

+ = above 5% significance level above the mean.
0 = no difference or within 5% significance limits.
− = below 5% significance level below the mean.
* = not enough cases available.

County were selected by interviewing informants, with care taken not to interview school administrators or teachers. At least three of the persons interviewed had to agree on the persons nominated. Note from the first column of Table 3 that for both the outstanding boys and the outstanding girls there is a consistent tendency to be significantly above the average of their group in every one of the general measures: intelligence, socio-economic status, the pupil indices of 1950 and 1954 which are a combination of personality measures, and the teachers' ratings of 1950. When we examine the scores of each of the many tests, measures of social status, inventories, rating scales used, and the indices developed from our original measures—whether taken by children or supplied by teachers in both 1950 and 1954—without exception, the outstanding persons of both sexes make scores which are above the 5-per-cent significance level. Since we did not obtain such a uniform or clear result with our measures of maladjustment, these results suggest that measurement of good performance and good adjustment presents fewer difficulties and perhaps requires less complex instruments than does the measurement of poor adjustment.

The other columns of Table 3 concern the poorly-adjusted groups in terms of our social criterion. For school drop-outs among the boys, the performance is significantly below the average level in all the general measures presented except for the 1950 Pupil Index. When, however, we study the many individual measures, there is much more variation than was found for the outstanding groups. For the girls who drop out of school, the pattern is essentially the same as for the boys. On individual measures, however, the drop-out girls are more variable than the drop-out boys.

For the delinquents, as shown in the third column of Table 3, the relations are still less uniform. Delinquent boys tend not to differ significantly from the normal population in intelligence, tend to be low in socio-economic status, tend to be equal on the 1950 personality measures, tend to be low on the 1954 personality measures, and are low in terms of teachers' ratings. For the delinquent girls, no significant relation whatever is shown for any of these measures. In terms of the individual inventories and tests, the pattern is also lacking in uniformity.

The number of emotionally disturbed boys was so small that we could not make meaningful comparisons with the normal population. But for the emotionally disturbed girls, the picture is one of higher IQ, but with respect to all other measures, no distinction from the remainder of the population appears. Note particularly that this holds for both the 1950 and the 1954 personality measures. Again when we analyze the particular measures in relation to this criterion, there are many puzzling relations.

What this adds up to, so far as the poorly-adjusted persons are concerned, in terms of outcomes may be a principle to the effect that dropping out of school and delinquency are the result of specific factors which combine in various ways. Being outstanding would, however, seem to be a more general manifold. Why does one end of the adjustment picture result in more uniform patterns of relations and the other not? One answer which is suggested by some of our data is that intelligence as measured operates as a more significant factor in adjustment at one end of the continuum than at the other. It may operate in either of two ways—by facilitating response to all the measures given, much as it operates with regard to the understanding of instructions in some tests which do not clearly involve an intellective factor; or by actually increasing the likelihood that the person will use whatever he has in the way of resources more effectively.

Cross-Validation from the 1955–56 Follow-Up to the 1957 Follow-Up. By an item analysis of the 1950 predictors in relation to the 1955–56 follow-up data, it was possible to devise instruments with which to check the prediction of adjustment on the 1957 cohort. These instruments are called item-extract scores. One instrument was made up for boys and another for girls from the teacher ratings. Then a second instrument for boys and a second for girls was made up from the pupil inventories. Next the items were selected out of the records for the 1957 cohort and grouped to give scores. This is a type of cross-validation from one follow-up to another follow-up and is subject to the limitation that the particular items are pulled out of their context in the instruments in which they originally appear. But this limitation applies to their use in both follow-ups. The correlations which were found are presented in the first half, Part A, of Table 4. It should be noticed that the score from the teachers' instruments predicts the combination score for adjustment very well and all aspects of

TABLE 4. Item-Extract Scores Based on 1955–56 Follow-Up and Criteria

A. With 1957 Follow-Up Scores	Combination Score	School Score	Informants' Score	Partic- ipation
Teacher				
Tsb—Boys	.63**	.64**	.50**	.44**
Tsg—Girls	.49**	.50**	.35**	.07
Pupil				
Psb—Boys	.36**	.46**	.23*	.33**
Psg—Girls	.12	.28*	.14	.30**

* 5% level $r = .22$ up
** 1% level $r = .29$ up

B. With Social Criteria	Out- standing	Drop- Outs	Delin- quents	Emotionally Disturbed
Teacher				
Tsb—Boys	+	−	−	*
Tsg—Girls	+	−	*	*
Pupil				
Psb—Boys	+	−	0	*
Psg—Girls	+	−	*	*

+ = above 5% significance level above the mean.
0 = no difference or within 5% significance limits.
− = below 5% significance level below the mean.
* = not enough cases available.

the other adjustment scores. For the girls the predictions are not so high and drop below significance so far as participation is concerned. For the pupil measures, the coefficients are not so high and the boys' instrument predicts at a higher level than does the girls' instrument with respect to every phase of the adjustment measures. In spite of the fact that the measures were devised specifically with respect to sex, and theoretically should give equivalent results for the sexes, both measures show substantially greater relations for boys than they do for girls, and thus reinforce our earlier statements about the possibility of differential patterns of adjustment for boys and girls.

The second part of this table, Part B, shows the relation of these extract scores to the various social criteria. For the outstanding persons they show a consistent tendency to be above the 5-per-cent level when compared with the average on each measure, a similar finding to that reported earlier. The dropouts also show a consistent pattern of being below the 5-percent level below the mean. There were not enough delinquent girls or emotionally disturbed girls or boys for us to be able to draw any conclusions about the relation these classes of persons have to the item-extract scores. But for the delinquent boys, the teachers' item-extract score separates the boy delinquents, whereas the pupil instruments fail to do so. It should be noted that when these predictors are compared with the results shown in Table 3, that the 1950 pupil index, which was the group of personality measures from which the item-extract score was made, does not discriminate delinquents. The results of Part B of Table 4 are consistent with the results which are shown in Table 3 for the instruments from which the item-extract scores were derived. We have not been able to validate these instruments on an independent group. For our present purposes they represent a cross-check which suggests further exploration of the possibilities of predictive instruments, especially the development and refinement of the teacher-rating techniques.

THE PREDICTION OF FUTURE ADJUSTMENT FROM PARTICULAR INSTRUMENTS

In order to answer our own questions about the psychological meaning of our predictors, we made a factor analysis of the predictors from the matrix of the intercorrelations between test scores and sought terms to describe the factor-loading patterns which seemed to emerge. We used Thurstone's centroid method with rotation to a simple structure by the single plane method. The results are presented in detail in our final monograph (3). Two adjacent year groups from the stratified sample were combined, giving four hundred cases for each analysis. Thus we have replications at various age levels, which interestingly enough showed very little difference in the patterns of loadings. For the nine-to-ten-year-old and the eleven-to-twelve-year-old groups there were available thirteen pupil measures and teachers' ratings from the 1954 data. Both age groups came out with the same pattern of loadings with family attitude in the first, socio-economic status in the second, adjustment (a factor consisting of four of our measures) in the third, and favorable attitudes toward experience in the fourth position. In this analysis a measure of intelligence, unfortunately, was not included.

More meaningful in terms of the total picture is the analysis at the fourteen-to-fifteen- and the fifteen-to-sixteen-year-old levels, which also agrees as to the loadings. Here we included background measures, pupil measures, and teachers' ratings from both 1950 and 1954. There were two sets of analyses, one in terms of the nine indices or the combined measures and the other in terms of the twenty-one original scores on the various instruments. For the nine indices, the adjustment factor comes out with highest loadings on three indices; next there appears a socio-economic or cultural status factor with highest loadings on three background factors; and third, an intelligence factor with high loadings on the intelligence quotient and the teacher index. For the twenty-one measures, we obtained the heaviest loadings on a factor which we call family attitude and adjustment, since it includes both types of measure. Next there is a factor called intelligence which includes IQ, responsibility, maturity, and similar measures. The third is a socio-economic factor which includes paternal education, paternal occupation, and home facilities. The fourth, a neurotic-adjustment factor, is almost wholly related to the psycho-neurotic items. The fifth is a participation factor based on interests and work habits; and the sixth, a favorable attitude toward experience based on open-end sentences, likes, and responsibility.

While it is impossible in the space available to consider the prediction of outcomes in terms of the specific scores on the many instruments we used, we may, however, in the desire to be of assistance to others interested in forecasting adjustment, freely associate about some of the measures used.

Intelligence. We were surprised at the emergence of the intelligence factor in a variety of our instruments (family attitudes, responsibility and maturity, adjustment) in spite of our attempts to minimize intelligence in selecting the personality measures. Next we were surprised that for prediction over a long time, the intelligence quotient seems to carry a heavy predictive load in most of our measures of outcomes. An exception is the 1955–56 assessment of outcomes for girls and the data on boy and girl delinquents. Our results can be interpreted either as showing how difficult it is to separate out an intelligence factor from the complex of personality characteristics with which we are dealing when we talk about adjustment, or as indicating how important intelligence is in the adjustive process. It should be noted that in a number of studies, adjustment at both the child and the adult level, whenever intelligence is included, emerges as a more significant factor than personality measures. In fact, because of its significance it is a common practice to control intelligence by sampling or pairing in order that other factors may emerge.

Social Status. There seems to be little doubt that adjustment outcomes bear some relation to socio-economic or social status. This has appeared in many earlier studies and appears in ours.

Since the various methods of measuring status are highly intercorrelated, and since information on status can be obtained readily, relatively simple measures can be included in any screening device. Socio-economic status seems to be an important factor in delinquency.

Responsibility. The responsibility scale used in 1950 and its revised form used in 1954 are related to adjustment whether measured concurrently or over a long period of time. Scales in this area differentiate the special groups and offer some possibility for further development (11).

Attitudes toward the Family. If we consider the family attitude scales, it is clear that the 1950 family attitude scale is superior to the 1954 social distance scale with respect to prediction over time. In our factor analyses both turn up with loadings in the adjustment factor. The literature gives substantial support to the principle that relations with parents in childhood affect later adjustment. In our data this seems to be particularly true for the adjustment of girls both in the normal and special groups.

Work Habits and Attitudes. The work habits and attitudes scale, which stresses chores performed and liking them, used in 1950, shows little relation to either concurrent or long-time adjustment. While theoretically the person's management of his own energy would seem to be related to adjustment outcomes, some new basis for measurement is necessary.

Interests and Activities. Our measures based on the range of interests and activities which have some relation to energy utilization similarly show almost no relation to the outcomes which we measured. Perhaps here also we need new insights.

Favorable Attitudes and Likes and Dislikes. The open-end sentence test, both the 1950 and 1954 types, showed some prediction of concurrent adjustment and seemed to be promising instruments. But in terms of long-time prediction, both proved relatively ineffective. A somewhat similar finding appears with regard to the likes-and-dislikes test. The 1950 edition, which consisted of a very large number of items, had more predictive value than the 1954 edition in which the number of items was sharply limited. There is some possibility that tests of this type are influenced by the momentary emotional state of the individual and hence do not have high predictive value.

Psycho-Neurotic Items. Much to our surprise, the psycho-neurotic items in the 1950 measures, which seemed to be promising and which have some literature supporting their use at the adult level, appeared to have little predictive value for final outcomes. It must be remembered, however, that we were working across an entire population of children, not in terms of a limited segment of disturbed persons. These items may not be appropriate for children and youth.

Adjustment Measures: Derived Instruments. The adjustment measure of 1954 and the adjustment and maturity measure of 1954, which involved an item-analysis of the 1950 instruments, show positive relation to our adjustment categories. However, this relation is not so close as we had anticipated; and it is clear that these measures cannot, in themselves, function alone as a screening device for locating individuals. But they may be of some value in combination with other devices.

Somewhat similar instruments are the item-extract scores, derived by item-analysis on terms of long-term rather than short-term outcomes. As shown in Table 4 these stand up reasonably well but need an independent verification on other groups with some check of their value.

Teachers' Ratings. With reference to the various teacher instruments, the 1950 check-list on responsibility seems to have some value. Some of the items from this measure were incorporated in the 1954 responsibility measure taken by the children and seem to hold up whether answered by pupil or rated by the teacher.

The nominations of the best-adjusted children and of the poorly-adjusted children, used both in 1950 and 1954, were essentially validating devices. They are of some value, but present such difficulty in scaling that they could hardly be formulated as a specific instrument.

The teachers' rating blank, which had twenty items in 1950 and ten items in 1954, seems to be an excellent instrument in terms of long-time prediction. The teachers' item-extract score derived from the 1955–56 material, consists very largely of items from this scale. Both in its ten-item form and the derived form it holds promise for development as a screening device. In view of the ease of administration, the short time needed for its use, and its predictive value, it might be well to study the possibilities of teachers' ratings as screening devices rather than to concentrate on a series of pupil measures.

CONCLUSION

Whatever the outcomes of this study, I feel that we have explored an important area and have moved forward. Could we begin again, we would have better design, more appropriate measures, and improvement in the method of analysis. The opportunity to examine the children came originally almost by accident and, because of the cooperation within the County, turned out to be unusual. Our project in a sense is one that itself changed with time, especially as we encountered the complexities of securing criteria for adjustment against which to measure our earlier data. The problem of the criterion is still the central problem. We have, however, explored several methods of getting information about the adjustment of persons from the community and of evaluating their relations to the community.

In thinking about the results, we must bear in mind that there are two problems: one is the demonstration of relations in the scientific sense and the other the prediction for an individual child. Generally we found positive relations between predictors and outcomes over a span of some years. True, there were some exceptions. In this sense the results are positive. But the problem of predicting for an individual is complicated by the presence of change over the years. Hence there are limitations to our power to say specifically that Johnny Jones who does poorly on our inventories and tests in 1950 will be making a poor adjustment five years later. Prediction can be done better for the child who does very well on our measures. It is, however, not an uncommon result in psychological studies that prediction is better for groups than for individuals.

When we look at the lives of some of the children, we see that there are factors operating over a long period of time which affect adjustment and which may make hasty generalization undesirable. As the person grows, he changes and the demands made upon him change. As he moves into new zones of experience, some of his earlier difficulties seem to get straightened out. For example, a fair number of adolescents were having difficulties in their homes and difficulties in school when they were first examined. But six years later, when they were accepting the responsibility of their own homes and their vocations and were really out on their own in the community, they seemed to be doing quite well in meeting their obligations and responsibilities. Putting them on their own brought out qualities which had not appeared to the same degree in their earlier school and home experience. It is difficult to determine how much of this is the result of growth and how much the result of actual change in the situation.

Working with the full range of the population rather than with specially selected groups, we have some feeling that normal persons work out ways of adjusting over time and possess a kind of resiliency that carries them forward. If our experience with this population does not make us optimistic about the technical aspects of prediction over a long time, at least it makes us optimistic about the capacity of normal—as distinct from clinical—populations to meet their own problems.

SUMMARY

1. This project examined children and youth between the ages of nine and seventeen years and then followed them up five to seven years later in order to study the prediction of adjustment and to explore the possibility of developing screening instruments that would sort out children with potentials for good and for poor adjustment. Because the children ranged from nine to seventeen years, additional information on the age relations of various measures was obtained.

2. The early measures given the children consisted of eleven personality and adjustment measures and three types of teacher ratings. Criteria of adjustment used five to seven years later consisted, first, of various measures of accomplishment in school and community, community reputation, self-rating, and an assessment of adjustment by expert interviewers; and, second, of a study of the children who were outstanding in their communities or who had difficulties, such as dropping out of school, delinquency, and emotional disturbances.

3. Some measures and items are age-bound in that they show consistent changes with age, whereas other measures and items are age-free or show no significant relationship to age. The age-bound types of items generally are found in the cognitive, intellective, skill, and knowledge area; whereas the age-free types of items are generally found in the emotional and personality area. Attitude measures occupy an intermediate position.

4. Predictors vary in their effectiveness in forecasting good and poor outcomes. In terms of the various criteria used for measuring later adjustment, groups are significantly separated

on the predictors. Viewed, however, in terms of individuals, the possibilities of prediction are more limited.

5. When a team of measures is used, prediction is increased. In such a team the intelligence measure carries heavy weight and personality measures carry less weight. Over time, teachers' ratings of the children have better predictive value than do personality measures.

6. Sex differences appear in the relations between predictors and criteria. An item-analysis from outcomes back to early predictors indicates also that the prediction of long-time adjustment differs for the sexes.

7. The prediction of outstanding adjustment seems to be done much more readily than is the prediction of inadequate or poor adjustment. Every predictor separates out the outstanding persons at later ages. The patterns of measures that separate out inadequately- and poorly-adjusted children show much more variation.

8. For the poorly-adjusted children in terms of social outcome, we get the best prediction for school drop-outs, next best for delinquents, and the poorest for the emotionally disturbed girls.

9. In reviewing the whole pattern of prediction, it seems unlikely to us that a very short screening instrument that will predict well into the future can be developed from our personality measures on the children. It is possible to develop an instrument made up of a combination of intelligence measures, personality measures, teachers' ratings, and measures of socio-economic status and home background, an instrument that will have substantial predictive value. But this is a large package in terms of time, cost, and professional help and it still does not meet the requirements of a compact instrument readily given to large numbers of children. There is a suggestion that the teacher-rating technique might be improved and become a screening device.

10. Factors that present difficulty in interpreting our data arise out of the changes within the person with age and the changes in the life situation the person faces. Some children who were rated poor earlier, moved up the scale and achieved satisfactory adjustment when they were on their own and freed from home and school.

11. The prediction of adjustment over a long period of time seems to involve many factors that are not present in short-term assessment and is, therefore, more difficult and complex than the evaluation of concurrent adjustment.

Bibliography

1. Anderson, J. E. "The Limitations of Infant and Preschool Tests in the Measurement of Intelligence," *Journal of Psychology,* VIII (October, 1939), 351–79.

2. ———. "Relations of Attitude to Adjustment," *Education,* LXXII (December, 1952), 210–18.

3. ———, et al. *The Prediction of Adjustment over Time.* (University of Minnesota, Institute of Child Development and Welfare, Monograph Series XXIII). Minneapolis: University of Minnesota Press (Scheduled for publication 1961).

4. Bayley, N. "Consistency and Variability in the Growth of Intelligence from Birth to Eighteen Years," *Journal of Genetic Psychology,* LXV (December, 1949), 165–96.

5. Beilin, H. "Effect of Social (occupational) Role and Age upon the Criteria of Mental Health," *Journal of Social Psychology,* XLVIII (November, 1958), 247–56.

6. ———. "The Prediction of Adjustment over a Four Year Interval," *Journal of Clinical Psychology,* XIII (July, 1957), 270–74.

7. Beilin, H., and E. Werner. "Differences between Well and

Poorly Adjusted Young Adults Based upon Psychologists' Ratings and Subjects' Self-Ratings," *Journal of General Psychology,* LX (January, 1959), 45–55.

8. ———. "Sex Differences among Teachers in the Use of the Criteria of Adjustment," *Journal of Educational Psychology,* XLVIII (November, 1957), 426–36.

9. ———. "Sex Role Expectations and Criteria of Social Adjustment for Young Adults," *Journal of Clinical Psychology,* XIII (October, 1957), 341–43.

10. Harris, D. B. "Parental Judgment of Responsibility in Children and Children's Adjustment," *Journal of Genetic Psychology,* XCII (June, 1958), 161–66.

11. ———. "A Scale for Measuring Attitudes of Social Responsibility in Children," *Journal of Abnormal Social Psychology,* LV (November, 1957), 322–26.

12. Harris, D. B., and S. C. Tseng. "Children's Attitudes toward Peers and Parents as Revealed by Sentence Completions," *Child Development,* XXVIII (December, 1957), 401–11.

13. Scott, W. A. "Research Definitions of Mental Health and Mental Illness," *Psychological Bulletin,* LV (January, 1958), 29–45.

14. ———. "Social Psychological Correlates of Mental Illness and Mental Health," *Psychological Bulletin,* LV (March, 1958), 65–87.

15. Stern, G. G., M. I. Stein, and B. S. Bloom. *Methods in Personality Assessment.* Glencoe, Illinois: The Free Press, 1956.

16. Tuddenham, R. D., and M. M. Snyder. "Physical Growth of California Boys and Girls from Birth to Eighteen Years," *University of California Publications in Child Development,* Vol. I, No. 2, Berkeley: University of California Press, 1954.

17. Woodworth, R. S., and Ellen Matthews. *Woodworth—Matthews Personal Data Sheet.* Chicago: Stoelting, 1923.

Roles of the Medical Disciplines
in the Study of
Personality Development

MILTON J. E. SENN

AT THE ONSET, I believe it important to define what I mean by medical disciplines. I have particularly chosen the word *disciplines* instead of sciences because I include branches of medicine in the group which are particularly clinically oriented, and while they may be following scientific methods they have not reached the status of the biologic or natural sciences. I am referring to the clinical subjects of psychiatry, pediatrics, and internal medicine, and include these with the preclinical sciences of physiology, pharmacology, biochemistry, and anatomy.

The fact that each of the other contributors to this volume is a social scientist is an indication of the predominant influence of the social sciences, especially psychology, in the study of personality development. That the medical disciplines also have had a role and certainly continue to have a natural interest in trying to understand the genesis of behavior and its meaning is the main proposition of this essay. My second proposition is that the proper study of the human personality merits the conjoined efforts of scientists in the social sciences and those in the medical disciplines, particularly when all are members of the same university faculty.

A review of the history of experimental psychology and of the medical disciplines mentioned shows that there has been in all of them a long-standing mutual interest in behavior as well as a parallelism in their development from biology, chemistry, physics, physiology, and philosophy. There have been numerous overlappings of interest and of influence of each of these sciences on the other since their beginnings. Many illustrations may be cited of developments in physiology which carried over into experimental psychology. Sensation, reflexes, nerve excitation, and brain function represent four fields of research in physiology which have become important parts of psychology. Such men as Bell, Purkinje, and Müller are as well known in psychology for their work in sensation as they are in physiology and in clinical medicine. The names of Helmholtz and Fechner are recognized for their contributions to the understanding of specific nerve energy and may be claimed as important pioneers in both medicine and psychology. And so down the list—from Pavlov and Bekhterev in reflexology, to the psychology of motivation by *its* protagonist Freud—continue the names of persons whose scientific interests spread beyond the boundaries of a single science. When Professor Edwin G. Boring of Harvard University was asked to pick out psychology's greatest names he answered that judging by the criterion of their persistent posthumous importance there were four great men in the history of psychology: Darwin, Helmholtz, James, and Freud. It is interesting to note that three of these great psychologists were men of medicine.

Helmholtz studied medicine in Berlin and for seven years worked as an army surgeon in that city. While practicing clinical medicine he was able to continue to lead an academic life in which he was particularly close to both Magnus, a professor of physics whom he succeeded, and Johannes Müller, professor of physiology. Helmholtz had great influence over such students as Brücke, who later became professor of physiology at Vienna; Ludwig, professor of physiology at Leipzig; and especially Virchow, who is still looked upon as one of the fathers of the medical discipline human pathology. William James was a graduate of the Harvard Medical School and taught physiology there. Sigmund Freud was stimulated by the aforementioned Brücke in his physiological laboratory in Vienna; it was there, by the way, that he made the discovery of the analgesic power of the cocoa leaves and thus was really the discoverer of cocaine. Freud took his M.D. degree at the University of Vienna and then began the private practice of neurological therapy in association with the well-known physiologist Breuer, who also worked under Brücke.

In the more immediate past, physiologists like those of Harvard, Professor Cannon and his associates, have concerned themselves with the interactions and transactions of different body systems and their influence on behavior. Cannon's concept of homeostasis has become well recognized and useful in clinical medicine, physiology, and psychology. The work of Selye, the pathologist, in endocrinology, particularly on conditions of stress, has also been fruitful in explaining some aspects of behavior. Davenport Hooker's interesting observations of the human embryo have become important to all students of behavior in demonstrating the early patterning and lawfulness of behavior. Although psychologists, like their forerunners the physiologists, have always had a great concern for the human being and his personality development and behavior, the beginnings of animal psychology by the way of

Darwin in the middle of the nineteenth century deflected frequently the interest of the psychologists from the human to animals of lower species. In the medical disciplines, animal experimentation has continued also to be an important part of research, but the influence of the clinical disciplines, particularly psychiatry, has fostered even greater interest in the behavior of man than in lower animals.

Without question the use of animals for the study of behavior has advantages and frequently must be carried out before any similar investigations can be carried out on the human being. However, there is reason to believe that Alexander Pope's observation, in his "Essay On Man," that the proper study of mankind is man is a valid one. Psychologists with long experience in comparative psychology are the first to admit that comparisons between behavior of animals under test situations transferred to man are frequently found to be incorrect and inappropriate. While there are species similarities occasionally in behavior, the differences remain great between one species and others. Psychologists and medical clinicians have learned to their sorrow many times that actions of such agents as drugs in animals may have quite opposite effects on the human subject. This is not to imply that all humans may be equated in their responsiveness to the same agent, whether it be physical, chemical, or social. A well-recognized clinical fact in medicine is that the child is not a miniature adult; his behavior responses are not only different as measured against the adult, but as measured against himself at different periods of childhood.

An example of attempts to apply psychologic theories to clinical problems of behavior in a laboratory setting with few positive results in understanding of human behavior is the usage of Pavlov's conditioned-reflex theory of mental disorders on animals under conditions carefully defined experimentally. While there is some resemblance between emotional disorders of human beings and those developed artificially in animals, Pavlov's theory, however sharply refined, remains largely an academic theory. Often experimentalists and clinicians have thought they were explaining clinical symptoms when they were merely transferring laboratory jargon into clinical jargon. On my visit to Russia in 1958 I saw this done frequently not only in neurophysiological and psychological laboratories, but in clinical situations in hospitals. One of the best illustrations of the absurdities that this transferring of jargon can lead to was afforded me by the Russians. I was told that most women in Russia deliver babies by natural childbirth using Pavlovian reflexology methods. On witnessing such a delivery, the natural childbirth method was exactly like that used in Great Britain and the United States, with the woman following instructions, learned prenatally, in how to breathe, how to relax, and how to use her hands in supporting the muscles of the back. While the words "First and second signaling symptoms" were used by the Russians to explain the maneuver, in actuality the natural childbirth procedure was exactly that of Read's of England, which makes no claim to usage of neuro-physiological mechanisms.

What the preceding example seems to show is that, although study of the human being is fraught with its own problems, nevertheless, there is great merit in trying whenever possible to study behavior of the *human subject* in the *context of his social milieu* in order that we may better assess and put into practice that information which one hopes will have practical value in helping *people*. The medical disciplines being charged with the study of the human being for the purpose of helping him overcome illness and of keeping him healthy have ready access to people as patients. There is a large reservoir of human subject material available for study not only by medical scientists, but also by social scientists. In addition to an abundance of human subjects, the many places where people come for medical care are available as laboratories where the studies of behavior may be made. For example, a social psychologist at Yale has recently studied the reactions of patients to their hospitalization. He studied their anxiety in the milieu where they were experiencing their apprehension, tension, and fears, i.e., in the hospital. Too frequently social scientists, especially psychologists, have taken theoretical statements and observations made by clinicians such as Freud and attempted to categorize and catalog such behavior, and then to segment off small particles of it and reconstruct it in their own laboratories for study. For example, Freud's theories and observations of the mechanisms of defense have been tested by psychologists not in situations where the mechanisms naturally developed but in laboratories where they were provoked artificially. As a result literally hundreds of studies have been made on such mechanisms as repression, but very little new knowledge or information which has been helpful in understanding human behavior or in helping sick people has come from these studies. Many psychologists who have engaged in this kind of research have sooner or later been impressed by its superficiality. The sort of things available for study in a laboratory seem not to be the sort of things that Freud was talking about in terms of repression. Thus a large body of experimental and quasi-experimental data has been accumulated which has no bearing on personality development because it does not touch the intensely personal issues of life which are repressible.

Something which does touch the repressible personal issues of life is psychoanalysis and research in personality development. Psychoanalysis is readily accepted today as an important clinical instrument. Equally true is a belief by many behavior scientists that psychoanalytic theories need further testing and validation. The importance of psychoanalysis to academic psychology and to other social sciences can be estimated by the great amount of investigation being carried on which is aimed at proving or disproving psychoanalytic theory. Since psychoanalysis is based on theories of genetic development, its implications for child psychology are particularly specific. For that reason psychologists working with children have shown a special interest in research aimed at testing or better understanding psychoanalytic postulates. Similarly, psychoanalysts working with children have become interested in the methods of academic psychology. Anna Freud, in 1953 at a Clark University convocation, recommended that psychoanalytic psychology be studied and validated through methods and techniques found useful in experimental and developmental psychology. It is my impression that by psychological study of children, solutions may be found to problems having to do with the nature of all learning, of normal adaptation and of maladjustment, as well as all other aspects of personality functioning. However, it is also my impression that no approach to the study of children can really be fruitful without using psychoanalytic theory and knowledge. The psychoanalytic method today is properly and most effectively used in a clinical setting, and, as stated earlier in this essay, it has not been successfully transferred to a laboratory or a laboratory situation. The proper laboratory of psychoanalysis must be the clinical setting where human beings come for a relationship with other human beings who have understanding of what will transpire emotionally between the persons involved in the interaction. This must be a one-to-one personal relationship and the purpose of the setting must be primarily to provide therapeutic help to some human being. Though study of what is happening in this clinical setting may be made— and this may be done rigorously and carefully enough to carry the name of research—investigators must always remember that it is action research, and hence more fluid and less controlled than in a laboratory where the design of an experiment may be followed closely and without deviation. For behavior scientists unfamiliar with clinical work, such research is less satisfactory not only because he feels uneasy by the fluidity of research in the clinical setting, but also because he cannot readily predict the direction and the results.

The most challenging as well as the most disputed component of psychoanalytic theory as it relates to children is its theory of psychosexual development, since this theory was derived from reconstruction of life events in the minds of adults. Psychologists and an increasing number of psychoanalysts are now in agreement that only the study of normal growing children can provide understanding of the nature of psychosexual development and its relationship to later personality development. The most available resource for the study of such children is a nursery school for the preschool child and the well-baby clinic for children of younger age. Psychoanalysts and psychologists today have become particularly interested in the beginning of life and in the equipment which the newborn baby has for reacting and responding to the world outside him. While it is rare for a medical school to have a nursery school within its structure, departments of pediatrics increasingly are having such preschool facilities in order to provide a laboratory for pediatricians and child psychiatrists. Every medical school does have some resource for the care of newborn babies and older infants. These nurseries, as well as the preschool and even the in-patient clinical facilities of a department of pediatrics, should be available not only to medical scientists and physicians-in-training, but also to behavior scientists, particularly psychologists. As I stated earlier, it seems to me that one of the major contributions of the medical disciplines, particularly in the clinical fields, could be the provision of clinics and clinical material for study by social scientists.

Another factor that bears on the advantages of making medical institutions readily available to the social scientists, thus permitting them to study human beings in settings which are more natural laboratories, has to do with the feeling of need to join with others in collaborative research that comes to most investigators with experience. As scientists become more and more sophisticated in their studies of the human personality, they tend also to become more and more inter-disciplinary in their interests. They come to the realization that their own frame of reference is highly specialized and permits only a narrow point of view. There is the wish to broaden their scope of study and to use tools which can more comprehensively evaluate the area under scrutiny. Since most investigators have been busy learning and becoming skilled in one set of instruments and using one system of conceptualization, they must call on colleagues in other disciplines either for advice and guidance in sharpening up their own methods, or as collaborative co-workers. Today there is no area that is as basically interdisciplinary in its form as medicine. Even medical education is now broadly based on both the biologic sciences and the social sciences. As the medical student becomes the physician he conceives of ill health as well as good health as being multi-faceted; he learns that in the practice of medicine he not only must think of things as having multiple etiology, but must include colleagues with different training and experience in his efforts at recognizing pathology and correcting it. With the inclusion of behavioral sciences in the training program of the physician, it has become easier and more natural for him to approach problems which require collaborative assessment than it may be for the psychologist, the anthropologist, or the sociologist who often by tradition is limited to the utility of his own field. Thus it would seem that in the development of large interdisciplinary teams to collect data on human personality development, the physician has a uniquely creative opportunity for fostering multi-disciplinary research, and possibly of being in the best position for guiding the synthesis of the divergent kinds of materials that have been gathered.

I am fully aware of the fact that when one speaks about creativity, giftedness of people transcends training. I am also fully aware of the fact that the medical scientist, especially in the clinical disciplines, often lacks the ability to design experiments with the clarity, accuracy, and rigorousness of the social scientist. The benefit to the medical personnel from such a union of scientific effort obviously is the training in methods of planning his own research more economically and effectively. Apt here is the well-known saying, "A clinician studies meaningful problems with meaningless methods, while the psychologist studies meaningless questions meaningfully." What I am advocating, then, is that in a university which has departments of social science and a medical school, there should be a collaboration of effort in research and in training. The idea that a university is the proper place for a correlated study of man is not new. At Yale we have been very sensitive to the idea ever since the setting up of the Institute of Human Relations. In 1927, the Dean of the School of Medicine at Yale, Dr. Milton Winternitz, with Dean Robert Hutchins of the Yale Law School, developed the idea of an institute to study human behavior by a group of scientists in medicine, social science, law, and economics. President Angell of the University, who will be remembered as a psychologist representing the Chicago school of functionalism, had independently considered the value of some kind of institute to study human behavior.

The plan of the Institute contemplated establishing a generalized and coordinated program of research and training of behavioral scientists. Over-departmentalization in the University had resulted in the tendency for scientists to specialize in ever narrowing fields. While something was gained from this, it was believed that there was also a loss of effectiveness, since many problems were approached too piecemeal and failed to add up to a comprehensive understanding of the problems studied. Moreover, important areas for investigation were neglected because they seemed to lie on the borderline between different sciences. Therefore, in the Institute emphasis was placed on interdisciplinary cooperation and a many-sided approach. In order that the Institute might represent the University's main attempts to correlate and integrate its intellectual resources in ways that would make its total strength most effective, it was considered essential to keep the Institute embedded in the University, lest it become another school or department with an independent identity. It was organized deliberately with the understanding that it would have no faculty of its own. Its senior professional personnel would be drawn from the teaching faculties of the University, with their primary appointments in the various schools and departments of the University. The administrative officers of the Institute were deans or department heads. Efforts were made not to duplicate University departments within the Institute, but rather to strengthen departments to the point where they could serve the Institute's needs.

The Yale Child Study Center, established in 1948, has a design similar to that of the Institute of Human Relations. Its aims are also identical, except that the focus is limited to problems of infancy and childhood. The Child Study Center's staff of senior research and training personnel frequently also have appointments in the clinical departments of the School of Medicine, especially Pediatrics and Psychiatry, and in the Graduate School Departments of Sociology, Psychology, and Education.

As was learned from the experiment in the Institute of Human Relations at Yale, however ideal the plan, integration and correlation in the field of human behavior research is difficult. The chief obstacles there seemed to be a lack of adequate means of communication between the scientists and hence a lack of understanding the data of one discipline by persons of other disciplines. Ideally there needs to be developed a new kind of scientist who is trained in more than one field, one who can speak a language which cuts across different sciences. That it is not easy to develop such multi-disciplined scientists we are aware, because even that experiment has been tried and has not always been successful in giving the person acuity in understanding his fellow-scientists and in translating the work in one field into insights which had meaning to others. Sometimes such scientists have had the experience of being handicapped much as the way Stephen Leacock said he was when recognized as a political scientist by one group of associates who were professional humorists, and considered a humorist by his colleagues in political science. Not being able to sit astride two stools very comfortably, he found himself falling between them. Despite this dilemma and the continuing inadequacies of the scientist trained in more than one field, there seem to be advantages to those persons and to those research endeavors where there are gifted persons with training encompassing more than one science.

The greatest obstacle to integrating and correlating efforts of research in the field of human behavior seems to be a distrust and fear of one's colleagues. There is a self-protectiveness, lest one expose his ignorance, which results in a projecting of feelings of distrust and fear onto the other fellow. Hand in hand with this goes the feeling of need to maintain strong barriers between university departments in order to protect the identity of each and to continue to win financial support for each. Where barriers have been removed between departments, financial and other support have been available in adequate amounts when the administrative officers have recognized the benefits which come from scientific teamwork. A striking example of this occurred in the last war when scientists working cooperatively applied scientific methods to every phase of fighting. In the name of an emergency, biologists, mathematicians, psychologists, physicists, chemists, physicians, and anthropologists worked together in teams and successfully solved problems presented by enemy bombers and submarines. Many of these scientists had been trained in graduate schools where the emphasis was on competence and cleverness within the scientist's own particular discipline. Out of the war came social and medical scientists who had a new respect for the special competence of their fellows.

Obviously, the beginning of collaboration and integration of efforts should come in the training period of all scientists. Certainly in a university there should be a mixing of students from the schools of medicine and the graduate schools of the social sciences and the humanities. Integration and cooperation and coordination can be achieved only by slow and natural growth. There can be no ordering or directing of people to integrate and coordinate. It has been demonstrated many times that as one person is attracted to another, each trusts and begins to understand the other. Before long there is a sharing of ideas, a pooling of effort, a joint appraisal of data. Both at the Institute of Human Relations at Yale and our own Child Study Center, the value of faculty study groups has been recognized as a preamble to establishing collaborative research or in setting up a new course of study called behavioral science. Such faculty study groups, meeting regularly for sincere and frank exchange of ideas and for criticism of one another's work, have led to some facility in communicating and in understanding persons from different disciplines. Meetings of younger faculty members particularly succeed because there is still time to experiment with one's own way of approaching problems. The older and more experienced investigator feels a

need to capitalize on his experience and training, and to follow the school of thought and methods with which he has
been particularly and especially identified.

In making a plea for a closer working relationship between
medical disciplines and the other scientists in the university,
I do so with the belief that much may be expected in the future
from such segments of medicine as pharmacology, physiology,
psychiatry, and pediatrics. The advances in pharmacology
which I refer to relate to the discovery of new drugs which
influence behavior and thus may be used to overcome deficiencies of metabolism and genetic endowment possibly responsible for many of our mental illnesses. The testing of the
action of drugs includes more than identification of clinical
effectiveness and pharmacologic toxicity. Clinicians and manu-
facturers of pharmaceuticals tend to be interested only in drug
action as it relates to modification of symptoms with a mini-
mum appearance of toxic side-effects. Clinical usage of drugs
in the hands of different physicians, and even in the same
hands but on different patients, has produced puzzling results.
For example, the effect of a drug may vary when it is used on
the same animal or the same patient in different social contexts; the effect may vary when the drug is used on the same
subjects at different times of the day and night. Too, an intra
and an interspecies difference has been noticed. As a result,
the use of the so-called tranquilizing drugs today is largely
empirical. This accounts for indiscriminate use of the drug
and the obsession to continue to seek different drugs with
different influences. If the medical clinician, the pharmaceuti-
cal manufacturer, and the pharmacologist could join hands
more frequently with the social scientist in preclinical planning of drug experiments and of assessing the results, I believe there would more often be a discovery of the specificity
of a drug's action.

In physiology greater understanding of the blood-brain

barriers will be helpful not only in the more effective use of drugs and other agents, but in explaining deficiencies of brain function. The hypothesis that schizophrenia may be due to interference with the functioning of serotonin in the brain is challenging. The discovery that lysergic acid diethylamide taken by healthy persons produces states of behavior resembling schizophrenia is equally noteworthy. The identification of a characteristic urinary excretion pattern for one form of mental deficiency (phenylketonuria) suggests that other patterns which are distinctive for other forms of mental pathology may be recognized. In further exploration of these ideas the social scientist could assist the medical scientist in innumerable ways. The sharpening of hypotheses, the proper choice of test subjects, the identification and control of variables, and the appraisal of data comprehensively are but a few examples of the kind of help social scientists may provide.

By the use of surgical techniques, the physiologist will unquestionably find rich dividends in research which follows the leads of Penfield in locating areas of the brain which are the storehouses of memory and the centers of learning, control, and integrative action. Although Freudian psychoanalytic theory will continue to influence psychiatry greatly, there is mounting evidence from the neurophysiological laboratory that morphology of the brain is in part responsible for the origin of mental attitudes and traits of personality. The fact that studies of brain morphology until recently dealt almost exclusively with post-mortem material handicapped investigators in understanding the relationship between brain structure and brain function in the live person. However, new tools, such as the electroencephalograph and electronic devices for stimulating different parts of the brain without surgery, are providing new information about live subjects. For example, Delgado at Yale, working with monkeys and human patients, has evidence which suggests that the functional organization of the brain depends on the presence of a number of centers which he calls neurological pools.* Each pool has a highly specialized function. Delgado believes that consciousness is not an indiscriminate function of the whole brain, but is dependent on the action of these pools, which consist of varying numbers of neurones. Stimulation of some parts of the brain causes confusion; of other parts, aggressive action; of others, sexual excitation; and of other parts, no response at all. This is presented as evidence that the neurologic pools are specialized areas, and, in support of the hypothesis that specific psychologic disease is due to a disfunction in specific pools. Tranquilizing drugs act differently for the different pools. Delgado's studies of behavior with mixed species of animals has led him to conclude that the interpretation of animal behavior, especially the affects, or what is commonly labelled as emotional behavior, is difficult because of the highly subjective bias of the observer. For example, he has correctly questioned whether a human observer can interpret aggression in an animal. While the behavior observed may be described and may seem to be aggressive, the judgment expressed depends on how the observer interprets what he has seen in terms of what he understands about human aggressivity. A number of investigators have tried to get around this human bias by having one group of animals observe the tested animals of the same species, both the tested and the observer animals being filmed by cinema for later analysis. Other researchers, at the conclusion of the period when they have observed the behavior of another person or of an animal, have been asked to write down their subjective feelings about the observed and his behavior. The use of multiple observers for the same test situation is being employed as a means of overcoming subjectivity in judging the attitudes, feelings, and

* Personal communication; unpublished manuscript, Yale University, New Haven, Connecticut.

actions of tested subjects. Delgado has also pointed out, as I have mentioned before, the great difference in morphology and physiology between the different animal species. He has identified intraspecies difference, and identified the influence in this of social factors. Apparently the social role played by an animal decides how he reacts to stimulation, and even to drug action. For example, a leader of a monkey group responds differently from the individual monkey who ranks low in the follower group. The leader also reacts differently tested alone from the way he reacts when tested in the presence of his mates. It is obvious that a social psychologist could be helpful to a neurophysiologist in assessing the influence, real and potential, of social factors in test situations.

The psychiatrist, using the sharper tool of psychoanalytic study of patients, will learn much more than is known today about the influence of early life experiences in forming later behavior patterns. In longitudinal studies of growing infants and children, and of families, he will join with pediatricians, psychologists, sociologists, and anthropologists to learn in an on-going fashion what happens to people, and how earlier experiences affect later behavior. Predictions made along the way may be tested. Such a long-term study of a small group of families, carried on at our Child Study Center since 1951, has produced a vast amount of biographical material which is difficult to assess because of the volume and the complexity of the data. Although the aim is to publish this material in various forms, including original biographical data for use of a variety of students, the great dividend which has been paid up to now from this research has been the learning it has provided to the participating scientists. Although each of these participants was experienced in his own special field and believed he knew much about human behavior as he saw it through his eyes of psychoanalysis or pediatrics or perhaps sociology, each member of the team found new insights not only into the nature of the human personality, but into the contributions his fellow scientists have to make to the understanding of the meaning of behavior.

The pediatrician who capitalizes on the new knowledge created by the psychoanalytic study of adults and children by participating in the longitudinal studies just described and by benefiting from the appraisals of behavior made by psychologists, physiologists, and pharmacologists, should be in a better position in the future to use that knowledge in the prevention of emotional difficulties of children and adults. Since the pediatrician deals with a relatively small group of families in our society, we will need to rely on other physicians and particularly educators to use the new knowledge and promote programs of child-rearing and education which will have built-in provisions for enhancing healthy mental development and for preventing mental illness. In order to do this effectively there needs to be much better means of communication not only between the professional persons involved, but also between the professional groups and the general public. It will do us little good if we have storehouses of knowledge about personality development which we cannot or will not put into practice in our family lives in the education and rearing of children. The social scientist is the expert in communication and thus is the key person to open up avenues which will facilitate the transfer of ideas and knowledge so that there may result the necessary implementation for the proper usage of what is known and considered valid information.

The importance of sharing knowledge can be seen in the problem of mental illness. I am sure that the problems of mental illness will never be solved by psychiatry alone, or even primarily, but by the united efforts of people in many fields—medicine, social science, education, and theology, even business and economics. As a matter of fact until business, especially that part of business known as advertising promotion, changes its ethics and its goals, it seems that we will not be permitted to put into practice the principles of mental health learned in medical and social science. Although it may be long before we can obtain cooperation between such seemingly separate endeavors as advertising promotion and psychiatry, surely we should not delay achievement of a closer cooperation between the schools existing in one university.

Close cooperation between a medical school in a university and other university departments is made difficult, I realize, by geographic separation. However, I am convinced that a medical school suffers from the isolation which usually exists between it and the other units. I would like to believe that not only is the proper study of mankind, man, but that the proper place to study man is in the university. Since the focal point of most of the training and research in a school of medicine has to do with man, it is only natural that a medical school should try to improve its perspective and broaden its vision of the concept of man by joining with others in the university who are directly or indirectly concerned also with human beings as individuals, groups, classes, and societies.

To conclude this essay, which stresses the relationship of the medical disciplines to the social sciences, a paraphrase of a statement made by Max Planck seems fitting: Actually there is a continuous chain from physics and chemistry to biology and physiology, and thence to the social, intellectual, and medical sciences, a chain which cannot be broken at any point if we are ever to have a proper understanding of man and his nature.

The Growth of Conscience

ROBERT R. SEARS

THE MEANING of *conscience* is not very precise in western culture, but the word has an approximate aura which nearly everyone understands. It refers to the standards of right and wrong, and the motivation to abide by these standards, that every normal person carries within himself. It is the incontrovertible dogma of obligation and responsibility, the not-to-be-argued-with moral sense, the deep-lying self-control of pleasure-seeking impulses. It is social man's most necessary nuisance.

Unlike the wassailing custom of Hamlet's Denmark, conscience is most honored by its observance, but it is most noted by its breach. The maintenance of good and proper conduct is so customary that we make little comment about it. A man must be *very* moral in the face of *great* temptation before he gains fame for virtue. But the overriding of conscience brings instant notice—and not admiring notice, either—from others and, most importantly, from one's self.

Indeed, it is this last fact that distinguishes control by conscience from other forms of social control. Phrases such as "a twinge of conscience" and "pangs of guilt" give the flavor of this uniquely human phenomenon. It is in the feelings that accompany the nonobservance of conscience's dictates that we see the clearest evidences of its existence in ourselves. The behaviors that follow such presumed feelings provide the surest measure of the existence of conscience in others.

If we may accept the notion that *conscience* is the name we give to internalized control and sanction, then there are three kinds of behavior that exemplify the process. One of these is *resistance to temptation*. Man is not born with a moral code—quite the reverse. He is born with a host of impulses that demand immediate gratification. He wants food, water, sleep, escape from pain, release of bowel and bladder tensions, and freedom to stretch his muscles. These demands may be cyclical or they may be contingent on special stimulation. Some are reciprocal. All are powerful, and the human infant can brook little delay without expressing complaint. His ways of getting gratification are primitive and egocentric, however, and would be quite unsuitable to organized social living if they were to persist into adulthood. Hence he must have imposed on him a process of socialization that brings his pleasure-seeking under control. He must learn to tolerate delay, to take into consideration the social consequences of his acts, and to use the more refined techniques of pleasure-getting that characterize the adult. These learnings apply not only to the primitive organic demands the baby has at birth, but equally to the new emotional ones that develop soon after. Aggression, dependency, competition, mastery, curiosity, and genital sexuality describe other demands which are as vigorous as those in the first list.

Socialization is never perfect, however, and the growing child retains strong vestiges of his earlier impulses and of his primitive modes of gratifying them. He is repeatedly faced with hunger, with deprivation of loved objects, with challenges to his desire for mastery of the physical world, and with frustrations of most of his wishes. In turn he is tempted to perform actions which the socializing agents—usually his parents —have forbidden. During his earliest years, the parents watch out for such tempting situations and serve as policemen to guard him from succumbing to the desire to do wrong. Eventually he must learn to guard himself, for parents cannot continue the policeman role indefinitely. He must learn the proper standards of right and wrong; he must be able to recognize his own impulses and deny himself the right to gratify them in forbidden ways. The degree to which he resists temptations at any given age is a measure of how rapidly and effectively his conscience is developing.

Nobody can resist all temptations. A young child, especially, has but imperfect recognition of the appropriateness of some of his acts. Some impulses are just too strong to be held in check. But this situation is not unique to children. All of us, at one time or another, are excited to do certain things that we have been taught are wrong. We learned early the principle that we must not hit smaller children, but as adults we sometimes take advantage of a weaker opponent. If we are males, we have always understood that we must not strike females. But lives there a man with soul so dead that he never has wanted to "crack" *some* woman on the head? We have been told that we must not make love to the wrong woman; we must not steal things that belong to others; we must not injure people. There are all kinds of things that, as children, we were told we must not do. Yet the inescapable fact is that, grown-up though we may be, we do have aggressive impulses, we do have sex drives, and we do have the desire to achieve certain of our own goals which are sometimes to be achieved only at the expense of someone else.

So we are faced with temptation. As good citizens, we usually resist it. But secretly, sometimes, we don't. We give in to

forbidden desires. This happens more commonly with children than it does with us adults. Ten-year-old George borrows
his eight-year-old brother's bike when his own back tire is
flat. He takes it for all afternoon without asking brother John's
permission. George goes off with his friends and has a fine
afternoon. But then he returns to find his brother moping
sadly in the back yard. John was going on a little fishing trip
that afternoon with *his* friends, but he didn't have his bike and
so he couldn't go.

What happens now? If we may presume that George has a
normal ten-year-old development of conscience, we can see
the second main behavioral exemplification of it. This is the
display of *feelings of guilt.* Conscience involves not only a belief as to what are right and wrong things to do and internal
control against wrong actions, but a power of sanction when
right and wrong have been committed. Moral righteousness—
a sense of conscious virtue—occurs when a temptation has
been recognized and overcome. A feeling of guilt—a punishment from within—follows a deviation.

George looks at his brother's sad face and recognizes that
he himself is responsible. He has hurt John. And that is forbidden. To be sure, he is ambivalent toward his younger
brother, and his guilt at having hurt him is alloyed with some
hidden pleasure. But it is just this gratification derived from
actually having hurt him which is forbidden. Breaking the
rule of "never take something without asking" was the first
deviation, but getting pleasure from the effects of wrong-doing
was a second. The cumulative effect of the two wrongs brings
on a feeling of guilt.

There is a third kind of behavior which represents *conscience,* but it is a more difficult kind to study. This is the positive side of the moral ledger, the matter of values and ideals.
It is obvious that life is not composed simply of avoiding
wrong. Every normal child absorbs motivation to achieve, to

be strong, to be clean, to be just, to be kind, to be successful. These qualities cannot usefully be conceived as only the socialized obverse of infantile iniquity. To be sure, they may have genetic roots in the same socialization processes that eliminate sloth, incontinence, greed, raging hostility, or others of the behavior qualities that must suffer modification from their original form, but the positive qualities become ideals to be attained in their own right. They are *the good*.

I think it is not surprising that the first two aspects of conscience (resistance to temptation and guilt) have been more studied than the third and more positive one. Much of what we know—or at least hypothesize—about the moral properties of human behavior comes from the clinic. Only recently have more experimental and more replicable investigations begun to examine these matters. Quite naturally, such studies have begun with the clinically obtained hypotheses. And clearly, the clinic historically has drawn its main clientele from the ill, the disturbed, the badly socialized. These are the ones who resist temptation too little or too much, and who are in trouble one way or another with their feelings of guilt. A clinic population does not draw so heavily from those who are achieving their own ideals. Even among the ill, the therapeutic focus seems to fall more intensively on lapses from grace than on failures to achieve the ideal.

Conscience is not a kind of homunculoid excrescence in the personality of man. It is simply a conceptualization of a certain class of behaviors. These characterize all people *in some degree*. They vary somewhat in content from person to person. Each child has his own unique ideals, each his special temptations, each his special deviations that are most conducive to guilt. To be sure, with a common culture there will be something in common among them, but there will also be differences, dependent on the specific conditions under which each child learns. Whatever the variation in content, however, all children gain some degree of inner control and sanction. The discovery of those child-rearing conditions which determine the extent to which these qualities are learned, or the rate at which they develop, constitutes one of the most important problems facing students of personality development today.

This matter has obvious practical importance as well as theoretical relevance. We are urgently in need of a better understanding of how to produce more people who have adequate consciences. By *adequate,* I mean suitable for everyday living in American society. Conscience can be too strong or too weak. If it is too strong, if it develops too rapidly and vigorously in early childhood, it represents a crushing of impulses, a deep inhibition that apparently spreads way beyond the behaviors that need control. A child with a too severe conscience develops values and ideals that are impossible to attain. He is a prig, a teacher's pet, a goody-goody—the kind of youngster who, in the third grade, stands always beside the teacher at recess and helps her frown at the rough boys or the giggling girls. In the sixth grade, he stays a moment after school and, with a knowing and intimate smile, says to the teacher, "some of these children don't work very hard at their lessons, do they, Miss Johnson?" As he grows older, he demands the impossible of others, too; he becomes a bigot, a priss, a prude. As an adult, he may demand conformity to forms of so-called morality from his fellows—forms of morality that are utterly unsuited to the needs and customs of the society in which he lives. Reformers, witch-hunters, nosy Parkers, and self-appointed guardians of the public morals have been a pain in the neck to Western society since its history began.

At the other extreme is the child with a too lenient conscience. He is recognizable by his capacity for overlooking the restrictions placed upon him by his teachers and parents and by the community in general. He is found among the youngsters who steal, who lie continuously and regularly, who beat up other children on the way home from school; these are the unsocialized, ineffectual youngsters of the community sometimes called the "bad boys." A child with a weak conscience is one who continues to require external controls—by policemen —and who develops little that can be recognized as adult values or ideals. In adulthood, he contributes himself to the shiftless, irresponsible, criminal part of the population.

These are the extremes. What we want in our society are people with adequate consciences. I must say, immediately, that we have no good way of knowing what is an optimum development of conscience. It lies somewhere between the extremes, but just where, nobody knows. Its strength is sufficient to keep conduct within the bounds of custom, to provide guilt feelings for only what society agrees is serious dereliction, and to sustain ideals and values that lead to culturally congruent achievement and productivity. These are time-worn clichés and help us not a whit. The question of what is optimum will be answered, in any case, only after we know something of the conditions that influence the strength and rate of growth of conscience.

The first and most primitive question that we must ask has to do with the consistency of conscientious behavior itself. Do the three aspects of conscience grow at equal rates? Are they of equal strength at any one stage of the child's development? Is it even accurate to speak of such a broad concept as "resistance to temptation," with the implication that a child has equal resistance to all temptations that may impinge on him? Does a given level of conscience development at one age predict an equivalent level at a later age? Is the child's conscience a measure of the man's?

Surprisingly, we know only a little of these matters. From our general knowledge of the role that the specific situation plays in determining any behavior—conscientious or otherwise—we may safely guess that correlations among different expressions of conscience will be less than perfect. In a recent study (5) at our Stanford University Laboratory of Human Development, we presented four-year-old children with five different test situations that provided measures of resistance to temptation. In each instance, the child was left alone, for twenty minutes or more, in a setting that offered temptation to perform a forbidden act. The degree of resistance shown was measured either by the latency of his succumbing to the temptation or by the seriousness of his deviation. The inter-correlations among the resistance scores ranged from zero to +.74, with a median of +.20 for the boys and +.28 for the girls. Neither of these medians was significant, but four of the ten correlations for the twenty-one boys in the group were significant at the .05 level of confidence, and three of those for the nineteen girls were at that level.

These results are not widely dissimilar from those obtained by Hartshorne and May in the studies of character development which they performed in New Haven schools in the 1920's (2). In those studies, a large number of school-age children were given thirty-two tests of honesty. In general, there appeared to be small positive correlations among the tests, although repetitions of the same tests commonly showed rather substantial similarity from one occasion to the next.

These findings have often been cited in support of the situational determination of resistance to temptation, but they may equally well be used to support the conclusion that there is nonetheless a small core of consistency. The question at issue is a quantitative one, not one for which an either-or answer is relevant.

Even psychoanalytic study offers little information about the longitudinal consistency of resistance (or guilt or ideals). Retrospective report, on the analytic couch or elsewhere, is notoriously unreliable. The fact that a prolonged analysis can provide evidence for a meaningful relationship between sequences of actions and their experiential antecedents tells us nothing about the actual consistency of behavior. If it convinces us that there is lawful determinism in the development of human behavior, that is all to the good, but every student of the science of human behavior makes an assumption of lawfulness anyway, with or without evidence.

In spite of the apparent strong influence of the situation in determining reactions to temptation, mothers of young children do get a generalized impression of the extent to which their own youngsters show signs of guilt when wrong-doing occurs. By the time a child is five years old, his mother is able to describe his characteristic emotional reactions to such experiences, and from this description it is possible to make a crude estimate—for example, a rating on a five-point scale—of how much guilt he shows. Such a rating can then be used as the consequent measure for which we can seek antecedents in the mother's child-rearing practices and attitudes.

Another procedure that permits a measure of high or low development of conscience is to select youngsters who are so extreme at one or the other end of the dimension that situational factors are virtually eliminated as determinants of behavior. For example, in one important study (1), a comparison has been made of the child-rearing experiences of two groups of adolescent boys. One group had so repeatedly demonstrated a lack of either resistance to temptation or guilt over wrong-doing that they were two-time losers with the law. The other comparison group was composed of boys similar to them in a number of ways, but with no history of conscienceless behavior.

Our question is, then, what child-rearing experiences appear to influence the rate of development and strength of conscience? Some years ago, in the winter of 1951–52, a group of us at Harvard undertook a study of 379 five-year-old children (4). All were in kindergarten at the time. We interviewed their mothers at some length, asking about their practices with respect to rearing their children. The mothers ranged in age from twenty-four to nearly fifty. They represented a very heterogeneous population. They came from two towns, the populations of which ranged from definitely lower class to lower upper class.

In asking these mothers how they brought up their children, we explored many areas of child rearing. We asked concerning the severity with which the children were socialized; this had to do with toilet-training, feeding, weaning, and the handling of hostility and aggression problems in the child's first years as well as in later ones. We asked how the mothers handled dependency relationships, what their reactions were to the child's expressions of affection toward them, how they dealt with the child's need for increasing independence. We asked also about their techniques of discipline, how much they used such techniques as isolation of the child (by sending him to his room) and the deprivation of privileges. (One of the things that we found interesting was that 96 per cent of this group of mothers had TV's, and 95 per cent reported that their best disciplinary technique was depriving the child of looking at TV!) We asked about physical punishment: how often they spanked the child. We did not say "how many times a day do you do it," but we implied that it wouldn't be surprising to us if they had done it every day several times. (And a few had, but not very many.) We asked a number of rather subtle questions directed toward discovering to what extent the mothers used withdrawal of affection as a device for punishing their children. For example, a child does something bad, and his mother looks sadly at him, saying: "I don't think you could have been thinking very much about how *I* feel!" Or "If you really loved me . . ." These various aspects of child rearing contained the "causes" of conscience-development that we were seeking.

Conscientious behavior itself was measured by the mother's report of her child's reaction to deviation. We probed carefully in our interviewing in order to secure detailed descriptions of the way each child behaved in connection with certain opportunities he had for misbehaving. For example, we asked for a full account of the child's history with respect to being aggressive toward the mother: of hitting, scolding, yakking, complaining, and doing other kinds of things that the mothers considered to be aggressive attacks on them. We asked for information about setting fires, about taking candy or other things which they were not supposed to take, of playing with other people's property without permission, and so on. All this was aimed toward getting the mother to think about occasions on which her child had failed to resist temptation. We then asked questions about how the child behaved when he didn't resist, whether he reacted to guilty feelings with confessions or apologies or efforts to make up for what he had done wrong, or whether he reacted with fear or angry attacks on potential punishers. One question was: "When he has deliberately done something he knows you don't want him to do, when your back is turned, how does he act?" Some mothers responded: "Oh, I can always tell! Whenever he comes in with this kind of hang-dog expression and sort of stands around and looks at me and has a kind of sad look, I know he's done something wrong." Others answered the question by describing the child's reaction of guilt in greater detail. For example, the child would come into the kitchen, when mother was busy getting something for dinner; he would stand around for a while saying nothing; then he would sidle over to her, with a shoulder-wiggling kind of behavior, and get up against her, clinging to her a little and saying: "Mommy, I love you. I love you, Mommy." And then, with tears beginning to stream down his face, he would confess something he had done that he shouldn't have done. Or perhaps the child would come in with an opening gambit of: "Mommy, I haven't done anything wrong."

In contrast to the preceding reactions, made to establish rapport, were the reactions of fear and hostility. A child would come to his mother and be petulant or irritable toward her. He might stand beside her if she were reading or writing and start mussing up her work. Or, if the mother was looking at TV, he might go over and snap off the switch, looking at the mother with a "What are you gonna make of it?" sort of expression. Still other children would definitely *not* do this, but would show signs of fear of punishment. One mother said: "Yes, I can tell when he has done something wrong. I can't find him all afternoon." Another mother described an occasion on which her child had hidden under the house from just after lunch until dinnertime; only when he failed to come to dinner did she realize that he was gone. Upon questioning him, she found that he had got into the garage, had begun playing with a half can of blue paint, and had chosen to sit on top of the car while he opened it. Having spilled nearly a half-gallon of paint on the car's hood, he had fled into hiding under the house for six hours—while the paint dried.

This kind of information permitted us to make an estimate of the degree to which a child had what we meant by conscience. If the child reacted by confessing, apologizing, or trying to make restitution, his conscience was considered high or strong. A low or weak conscience was indicated by hiding or becoming aggressive. We estimated the amount of conscience for each of the children in the group and then tried to discover with what child-rearing practices a high conscience was correlated. First of all, it should be mentioned that the children who had high consciences were those who had been relatively dependent toward their parents during the preceding two or three years. The mothers described them as seeking parental attention unnecessarily, as being disturbed by having the parent go out in the evening, and as having a tendency to cling to the parent.

So far as child-rearing practices associated with high conscience were concerned, there were three main kinds. First, the mothers of the children with the strong consciences were ones whom we characterized as being nonrejecting; they were the "accepting" mothers. They were the ones who liked their children, who appeared to have never had any reluctance to accept them as members of the family, who did not find the children competitors with themselves for their husbands' favors or their husbands' interest, and who did not find the children continuously burdensome.

Second, the "high conscience" children were ones who had been disciplined more usually by procedures which were love-oriented. Basically, these techniques are based on withdrawal of love as a disciplinary device. They include the separating of the child from the parent, by either physical or psychological means, in such a way as to prevent him from getting the amount of attention and affection to which he is accustomed. This may mean sending the child to his room, or it may mean the kind of psychological separation that I was implying in the description of the mother who said: "I don't think you really have thought about how *I* feel," or "I don't see how you could do this sort of thing if you really cared for me." Or the mother who simply looks at the child and feels so bad about what the child has done that she gets tears in her eyes and turns away. The turning away need not be physical: it may be the withdrawal of love simply by changing the facial expression a little bit, "coldening it up" somewhat, as much as to say: "Well, I guess we two are not together. You are you and I stand here sadly." This is a kind of psychological separation.

These love-oriented techniques are to be distinguished from material-oriented ones such as physical punishment, deprivation of privileges, or, on the positive side, the use of tangible rewards. Love-oriented methods (including sheer praise as a reward for good behavior) are very different from the kind of discipline that's represented by "Come here and get over my lap!" Or "Bring me that hairbrush!" Or "You can't have dessert or look at TV!"

It is interesting to note that the positive relation of love-oriented techniques with strong conscience occurred only among those mothers who were judged, from the tone of the whole interview, to be warm and affectionate toward their children. Among mothers who were cold—who did not normally give very much love—withdrawing love had no effect on conscience. Apparently one cannot withdraw what isn't there.

A third kind of maternal behavior that was positively related to high conscience was the use of *reasoning* in connection with discipline. Reasoning is exemplified by such a statement as this: "Well, when he does something wrong, we sit down and we talk about it, and I try to explain to him how I feel." This kind of treatment probably brings in some withdrawal of love, but she will go on to say: "I tell him what other people do, and how and why it spoils our house, or why it isn't good for other people, or why it isn't good for him. I try to talk it all out with him and let him talk about it so that we can understand one another." (This "understanding one another" *can* mean smothering the child into believing that he thinks the same way his mother does!)

These four factors are the main ones that seem to be related to the development of conscientious behavior at age five.

Now let us consider the findings from adolescence. There are two studies to be cited: one, the study of a group of normal adolescents; the other, a study of adolescents who by no means could be considered normal. The first was an examination, by Peck (3), of the child-rearing practices of parents in an anonymous midwestern town. The children were observed over a period of several years. This study has a distinct advantage over the one we did in Massachusetts because the measures of the children were obtained quite independently of those of the parents; thus there was less risk of distortion. Peck obtained an estimate of the adolescent's resistance to temptation. He found two major parental behavior qualities that were correlated with high resistance, i.e., with what I have been calling strong conscience. The first of these was the consistency of parental control in the family life. The parents behaved much the same way all the time, providing stable disciplinary relationships with the child through his growing period. The second quality was one of high mutual trust and esteem among the family members. This quality has appeared, in one way or another, as a correlate of "good"—well-socialized—behavior of children in a number of studies in recent years.

So much for normal adolescents. The other study, by Bandura and Walters of Stanford (1), used the procedure mentioned earlier for getting a measure of conscience, namely, selecting a group that *lacks* it. This study sought the child-rearing practices correlated with bad consciences—poor, ineffectually developed consciences.

Bandura and Walters selected a group of very difficult boys. In a study of twenty-six fifteen- and sixteen-year-olds who were on parole for their second major offense against California law. They had been paroled either to the county supervisor or to the California Youth Authority; in each case the offense which had been committed on both occasions was one which was violent and destructive. These involved smashing automobile windshields for sport, or taking a stolen car up on a high hill, setting it to go over a cliff and then jumping out and letting it go over. There were instances also of rape and sexual promiscuity. These destructive and sexually malignant individuals were the "lacking in conscience" group. Their whole history, obtained not only from court records but also from both the parents and the boys themselves, showed a very low capacity for resisting temptation. Interestingly, projective tests given the boys at the time of the study showed almost no evidence of guilt feelings, either.

As a control group, twenty-six other boys were selected from the same schools and neighborhoods. They had the same teachers and were of the same social class. Nearly all boys in both groups were American-born, white, and Protestant. In other words, the two groups were quite similar to one another in terms of conventional demographic variables. But the control group of boys appeared to have normal conscience development. Both mothers and fathers were interviewed at length with an interview similar to the one with which we had studied the child-rearing practices of the mothers of kindergarten children.

Comparison of the parental reports of the two groups indicates the factors associated with inadequate conscience development. One of the most significant factors that appeared in reports about these badly socialized adolescents was a variable that had also been prominent in our study of the five-year-olds. This had to do with dependency. The young children who had strong consciences tended to be more dependent than those with weak ones. Now we find, in these delinquent adolescent boys, there was an almost pathological degree of *nondependence*. This is corroborative of the earlier findings, but what is more significant is what the parents said about the child-rearing attitudes and practices that went along with the development of this nondependence. The parents of the delinquents reported very high punishment for dependency supplications. In the beginning the children apparently had developed, as any normal child does, a strong need for affection and nurturance, of wanting care from the parents. Normally, mothers respond to these supplications for care and nurturance by giving affection, by helping—"Well, if you can't tie your shoes, come on and I'll tie them for you." When the child comes to them and says, "Mommy, I love you!" the mother tends to turn to the child and say, "Well, I love you, too." If the child asks the mother ten unnecessary questions, she tends to answer them while she goes on with her reading or cooking or whatever she is doing. She knows that he doesn't really want a careful answer; what he really wants is just to have her touch him, verbally, keeping in contact with him. The history of these adolescent trouble-makers clearly revealed that from an early age all such supplications of these children had been rebuffed. Questions referring to these matters were asked: "What about when the boy came and wanted to give you a hug or wanted to sit on your lap? What about if he wanted to kiss you?" This was a question referring to the earlier period of the child's life, when he was four, five, six, seven. The characteristic reaction of the father of one in the delinquent group to this question was turning the head away, frowning, looking rejective, and saying, in effect: "Aw, I never went in for that kind of sloppy stuff. This makes me very uncomfortable. I don't like this kind of business. Kids are supposed to grow up and stand on their own feet. You're not supposed to go around kissing and slobbering all the time." These fathers appeared to be unable or unwilling to engage in a warm and intimate relationship with their sons. Thus these children developed a high dependency anxiety.

Second, there had been, for the delinquent boys, a high use of material-oriented discipline. Physical punishment had been somewhat higher than it had been for the control group, although this difference was not as great as the difference in the use of deprivation of privileges and the use of tangible rewards. When the child was good, he was not praised. Rather, he was given a nickel or a penny or a gold star or a piece of candy, or he was told: "All right, now you can go to the movies alone." He was given some privilege, or, when he was bad, some privilege was taken away from him.

Third, there was a *low* use of reasoning, just as there had been a *high* use of reasoning with the five-year-old children who had well-developed consciences.

The remaining variable to be considered, which was important for the five-year-olds, was acceptance. It would be very difficult to get a reliable and meaningful measure of acceptance and rejection by the parents of these delinquent boys. The unhappy parents had had their sons in and out of court, in and out of jail; they had so often been awakened at night by the police coming to tell them of some desperate and terrible thing that any rejection the parents might express when the boys were in their teens would be all too realistically deserved. One would not be able to tell, at that late stage, how rejected the children had been at the earlier period.

These various findings about early childhood and adolescence provide a fairly consistent picture of the child-rearing factors related to the development of conscience. There are doubtless many other influences from within the family that help determine how much resistance to temptation a child gains, and how severe are the guilt feelings he suffers from deviation. It is to be hoped that future investigations can discover these and can more precisely delimit and define the variables to which these present researches have initially pointed.

The research task will not be easy, however. What is reflected in current evidence as a low consistency of performance from one resistance situation to another will represent a serious theoretical as well as a methodological hazard. Our best interpretation of these facts is that the great variety of variables, which we lump under the rubric *situational*, is responsible for the great variations in response. Such matters as the degree of risk involved, the strength of incentive presented, the amount of previous rewarded or nonrewarded experience in succumbing to temptation, and the symbolic significance of nonresistance as a form of defiance are surely important. The strength of each of these factors must vary more or less independently not only for each child but for each situation. Indeed, when one contemplates all the possible determinants of a single act of wrong-doing, it seems miraculous to discover that there is any consistency whatever in a child's character.

There is a little, however, and it is this little that seems to be accounted for, at least in part, by the child-rearing experiences so far discovered. It appears that the first stage in the growth of conscience is the development of a reasonably normal emotional dependence of the child on his parents. Then, if the parents are warm and affectionate, if they maintain an atmosphere of mutual trust and esteem in the family, their stable and consistent usage of love-oriented techniques of discipline produces self-control. One may hazard the guess that the effectiveness of such training methods stems from the fact that the normally dependent and loving child must devise habitual ways of insuring the continuation of his parents' love. An obvious procedure is to adopt the parents' values and ideals, their controls and restrictions, as a part of the child-self's own charter of conduct. The more they reason with him about his past transgressions, the easier will be this task, for reasoning provides the labels and the short-cuts of understanding so necessary for efficient learning. In fine, the child's own conscience becomes the self-protective absorption of the consciences of the parents themselves.

Bibliography

1. Bandura, A., and R. H. Walters. *Adolescent Aggression.* New York: The Ronald Press Company, 1959.
2. Hartshorne, H., and M. A. May. *Studies in Deceit.* New York: The Macmillan Company, 1928.
3. Peck, R. F. "Family Patterns Correlated with Adolescent Personality Structure," *Journal of Abnormal & Social Psychology,* LVII (November, 1958), 347–50.
4. Sears, R. R., E. E. Maccoby, and H. Levin. *Patterns of Child Rearing.* Evanston: Row, Peterson, & Company, 1957.
5. Weinberger, G. "The Measurement of Resistance to Temptation." Unpublished Master's thesis, Stanford University, Palo Alto, California, 1959.

Resource Mediation and Learning
by Identification

JOHN W. M. WHITING

THIS paper represents the current state of a theory of identification, or, more properly, learning by identification, that has been developed at the Harvard Laboratory of Human Development during the last ten years. It is impossible to give proper credit to the various members of the staff who have contributed their ideas to the current formulation.* On the other hand, certain former and present members of the staff will disagree with some of the assumptions stated here and should not be held responsible for them.

Many of the ideas presented here may have a very familiar ring. We, of course, have drawn heavily upon Sigmund and Anna Freud and many of the Neo-Freudians, as well as the

---

* R. Sears, P. Sears, E. E. Maccoby, H. Levin, E. Lowell, W. Lambert, W. Allinsmith, B. Whiting, and J. L. Fischer. Forerunners of this formulation have been presented in Whiting and Child (3), Sears, Maccoby and Levin (2), and in Maccoby (1).

behavioristic theories such as those of Hull, Miller and Dollard, Mowrer, and the cognitive theories of Tolman and others. We will make no attempt in this paper to give proper citation for the sources of these ideas.

Although we do not presume that learning by identification occurs only in the home or that a child identifies only with his parents, we have focused on this relationship to build our model. This has led us to consider in detail the types of interaction between a parent, particularly a mother, and a child that may occur during the course of socialization. Furthermore, we have limited our interest to the learning of social roles rather than the skills for coping with the nonsocial environment.

The term "identification" has been used in many ways. We do not wish to become involved in taking a stand on this or that precise meaning for the term, but rather we would like to use the term to refer to the general process by which a person learns the role of another by interacting with him. Although trial-and-error learning and direct tuition by socializing agents play an important part in the learning of social roles, we are concerned here with the more indirect, unconscious, unintended, and "incidental" aspects of this process. It is our purpose here to state some hypotheses concerning the conditions which affect such learning. We wish, if you like, to specify the parameters of learning by identification.

We would like to introduce here the notion of the control and administration of resources as a set of concepts by which social interaction can be described and which we believe to be crucial determinants of "learning by identification." By a "resource" we mean anything that a person (in this case a child) wants. Common resources are, for example, food, water, sex, optimum temperature, rest, privilege, information, freedom from restriction, freedom from pain, as well as some very important derived resources such as love and praise.

THE VALUE OF A RESOURCE

We also presume that any given resource may have a vary-ing *value*—the value of a resource being the degree to which the person in question wants it. The value of a resource at any moment will, of course, depend upon a person's previous ex-perience with the resource (derived wants) as well as his state of physiologic need at the moment. In other words, the princi-ples of learning and perfomance are applicable to the value of a resource under the assumptions (a) that the consumption of a resource is reinforcing, that is, it heightens the possibility of this type of behavior recurring and (b) that the withholding or deprivation of a resource is motivating. Thus, the value of a resource can be determined from both previous reinforce-ment and the current strength of relevant drives.

In addition to the value of a resource deriving from the number of past reinforcements and current primary drive state, we believe that insecurity with respect to the availability of a resource enhances its value. A resource that is available whenever one wants it is perceived to be of little value com-pared to one that is sometimes available and sometimes not. Thus the primary value of air should be greatly enhanced for those trapped in a mine disaster. Although air is of great pri-mary value—its absence is highly motivating and its consump-tion highly reinforcing—in ordinary living there is little if any insecurity with respect to its availability; thus, it has little, if any, enhanced value. The well-known economic principle re-garding the value of scarce goods provides another example. Furthermore, psychological research showing the effects of aperiodic reinforcement is relevant to this hypothesis.

We can now define more precisely what we mean by the value of a resource. First a resource is valued to the degree that its absence increases motivation and consumption provides satisfaction. Second, the value of any resource may be increased or enhanced by insecurity—threats that a resource already available may be taken away or that desired resources may be withheld.

ACCESS TO RESOURCE

Having defined a resource and stated some assumptions about its value, we are now in a position to discuss the control of a resource as it relates to social interaction. Although a child may have *direct* access to and control over some resources such as air, or perhaps rest, there are many resources, particularly when he is very young, that he can obtain only through others. That is, he can obtain them only by such acts as *begging, bargaining, attacking,* or *obeying.* We would like to refer to this relationship between a person and a resource as *indirect control of a resource.* Thus, in the parent-child diad or interaction, the parent has direct control over many resources which the child controls only indirectly through the parent.

RESOURCE-MEDIATION

With this notion of indirect control in mind, one can define socializing agents as resource mediators or resource administrators. In mediating a resource, the socializing agent may either *give* a resource, *withhold* it, or *deprive* the child of a resource that he already has. Thus a parent may provide the child with food, solace him, or praise him (resource-giving). She may refuse to give him dessert, restrict his freedom, or withhold her love (resource-withholding). Finally, she may spank him, criticize him, or take away a privilege that he has previously enjoyed (resource-deprivation). It should be noted that physical punishment is here viewed as depriving the child of the resource of freedom from pain.

In addition to the mediation of resources by withholding, depriving, or giving them, a socializing agent may threaten to withhold or deprive or promise to give. Threats seem to have the effect of enhancing the value of a resource by arousing insecurity, whereas promises have a reinforcing effect by reducing insecurity.

CONTINGENCY OF MEDIATION

A socializing agent may mediate resources for a child for different reasons or under different contingencies. Although they may in many instances overlap, three contingencies which have quite different effects on the process of identification may be specified: (1) *child-need contingency,* which refers to the care-taking function of the mediator; (2) *child-behavior contingency,* which refers to the teaching or disciplinary role of the mediator; and (3) *mediator-need contingency,* which refers to "parent-centered" in contrast to "child-centered" interaction.

Now that a vocabulary for the description of social interaction has been presented, some hypotheses are in order concerning the relation of social interaction, or as we would put it, resource-mediation, and learning by identification. To be more precise, we are concerned with the conditions under which a child will learn the role of a resource mediator. The process, we believe, may be divided into five stages.

COGNIZANCE

The first step in the process of identification in our theory is learning to predict the behavior of a resource mediator. In order to perform efficiently his own part in a diadic interaction, a child must be able to predict accurately the behavior which is reciprocal to his. We would like to refer to this as "cognizance," since we believe it may be governed by the laws of cognitive rather than instrumental learning. As Edward Tolman would put it, a mother's behavior is an important part of a child's cognitive map and he learns very well to match his behavior with hers. He will learn to turn his head when she offers him the breast or bottle, to arch his back when she stoops to pick him up, and eventually even to stop kicking when she is changing his diapers.

To have cognizance of the role of the other, although we believe it to be a precondition to the process of identification, is not in itself enough. Experimental evidence of the amount of savings from latent learning is ambiguous on this point. Some experiments suggest that there is some, others that there is none, or at most very little. If a child has interacted to a considerable degree with another person and is able to predict very accurately what he will do, the evidence seems to be that he will be able to learn the role of the other somewhat more quickly, but not very much more, than a child who has never been in such an interaction. Furthermore, there is no indication that he will have any desire to play the role of the other. Our hypothesis is that under these circumstances, if given a free choice between performing his own role or that of the mother, his own role will be clearly dominant, and he will choose it.

If we assume that cognizance follows the principles of cognitive learning, the clarity and accuracy of cognizance will be a function of the vividness, frequency, and consistency of the behavior cognized. The mediation of highly valued resources certainly will be vivid to the child and in many instances both frequent and consistent. Presumably these latter two components will vary both with a particular mediator and with the type of resource mediated.

STATUS-ENVY

Since cognizance provides the ability to predict the behavior of others, but neither the wish to perform such behavior, nor much savings in the ability to perform it, we will have to search for another factor by which we can predict these latter events. We have chosen *status-envy* as a label for this. If a child perceives that another has more efficient control over resources than he has, if, for example, he sees other people enjoying and consuming resources of high value to him when he is deprived of them, he will envy such a person and attempt to emulate him.

From this it follows that a child will not envy the status of the person who gives him resources because in this instance he, the child, is the consumer of the resource and already occupies the envied status. He will, on the contrary, envy the status of those resource mediators who withhold resources from him, deprive him of resources that were formerly his, and consume or enjoy these resources in his presence. This process may be termed *envy of resource mediator.* If the resource mediator withholds a resource from a child and gives it to a third person, this third person will occupy the envied status. Special instances of such a state of affairs are sibling and oedipal rivalry.

We predict that as soon as a child comes to envy a status he will attempt to play the role associated with such a status. Although sometimes he may be successful in this, more often than not he will be unable to play the role. His own size and immaturity, added to cultural rules which often restrict a child from performing adult roles, militate against this. The child's first attempts to open the icebox door, get a bottle, warm it, put the nipple on, and suck from it, are likely to fail. Furthermore, he is very likely to be scolded for trying.

Although status-envy in itself does not provide a means for learning the role of the other, it does give a means for predicting which role a child will prefer if given a free choice. We are assuming here that he will prefer to try to perform the role of the most envied status even though he has not yet instrumentally learned it.

COVERT PRACTICE

We are now ready to state our major postulate with respect to learning by identification. The more a child envies the status of another with respect to the control of a given resource, the more he will covertly practice that role. By covert practice we mean that he will indulge in fantasy in which he sees himself as the envied person controlling and consuming the valued resources of which he has been deprived. It is this fantasy of being someone other than himself that we would like to define as identification, and we would like to make the explicit assumption that such fantasy-role-playing will produce appreciable "savings" when the opportunity arises for him to perform overtly the coveted role.

Stating our theory as we have presented it thus far in terms of the parent-child model, we would predict that during early infancy while the mother is primarily nurturant, that is, doing her best to give the child everything he wants, *his* will be the most desired status, and he will see himself in fantasy as receiving resources from an all-giving mother. Thus, he will identify with himself. His covert practice of a role will be consistent with his own overt performance. The amount of nurturance given him during this period will affect only the value of the resources given and thus is a necessary but not a sufficient precondition for identification.

It is only when the mother begins to socialize the child, however, and for purposes of controlling him and training him begins to withhold or deprive him of resources, that the process of identification begins. It is then that he perceives that she has more efficient control of resources, begins to envy her status, attempts unsuccessfully to perform her role, and ends up with a new kind of fantasy in which he sees himself as the mother, rather than as the child. It is at this time also that he may envy the status of other figures. When resources are given by his mother to his father, or to a younger sibling, in preference to him, he will envy these statuses, as well as the status of his mother. We would predict that such persons will appear in his fantasies and that he will overtly attempt to perform their roles and, if unsuccessful, covertly practice them.

Available evidence seems to support this position on the development of identification. It is consistent with studies which have shown identification with the aggressor. It is also consistent with the numerous studies that have shown denial of love to predict identification, as measured by the strength of the superego, better than warmth and nurturance. (2,3).

OVERT PERFORMANCE

We have already stated that a child will attempt to perform overtly the role of an envied status, but that he will more often than not in early childhood be unsuccessful in doing so, and that under these circumstances he will covertly practice this role. This covert practice will have the effect of both increasing his latent skill in playing this role and his desire to do so. As a consequence, he will be ready to perform the role whenever the appropriate occasion to do so arises, and he may, indeed, even persistently seek to perform overtly those roles inappropriately, that is, in the face of negative reinforcement. Although we presume that success or failure in the overt practice of a role will certainly modify it according to the principles of instrumental learning, we do assume that persistent covert practice of a role will make it more resistant to such modification.

ASCRIBED STATUS

If a child were permitted by the rules of his culture to perform the roles of any status he wished (i.e., any envied status), the process of socialization might be quite different from what it is. Such is not the case, however. Every society has rules of status occupancy which may be quite at variance with the desires of a growing child. Rules based upon the sex and age of the child are particularly important. A child cannot act either "like a baby" or "like a grown-up." A boy cannot be a "sissy," nor a girl a "tomboy."

The rules of status-occupancy taken together with status-envy have some interesting consequences. Suppose a mother has had control of all the valued resources for a boy. According to our theory, he will envy her status and strive to perform her role. His mother, however, is a woman and part of the behavior that he desires to emulate is sex-typed and forbidden. Such a boy finds himself in dire conflict. He has a number of alternatives. He may practice feminine-role behavior despite the sanctions against it, or, if the sanctions are too compelling, inhibit his impulses to perform such behavior; but, our theory would predict, he would continue to practice covertly and would thus have a feminine self-image. Finally, if he is lucky, he may find a male who has control of resources of sufficient value to him that he can accept him as a model and thus learn appropriate masculine roles. A recent study carried out at the laboratory suggests that male initiation rites at puberty may perform this function (4).

Age-grading also leads to conflicts in the socialization process. Cultural rules typically permit a child the indirect control of resources at an early age, and deny him the right to such control at a later age. To get what he wants by crying is denied to an older child. This may, and often does, lead to the envy of his own previous status and to the covert practice of roles associated with it (regressive fantasies). Again, the process of socialization can be successful only if he is able to learn efficient direct control of resources (independence) required of older children so that he no longer envies infancy.

LATENT IDENTIFICATION

From persistent covert practice, and from the cultural rules regarding ascribed status presented above, it follows that the desire to play many roles of envied statuses may remain latent for many years. It has often been noted that a mother will frequently respond to her first child exactly as her own mother had treated her, even though she had not been aware of practicing such behavior, and, in fact, may even have vociferously sworn that she was going to bring up her children differently. This suggests, of course, that covert practice of envied roles may often be disguised and unconscious. It suggests furthermore that the measurement of latent identification may be very difficult and require the astute use of projective tests and other such means of discovering tendencies of which the subject is not consciously aware.

FAMILY STRUCTURE AND IDENTIFICATION

Cultural arrangements regarding the degree to which resource mediation is focused on one member of the family or distributed among many, and customs regarding the differential mediation of different resources should have important effects on both the strength and content of the roles learned by identification. We would assume that where there is a high concentration of resource-control and mediation in one socializing agent, there will be a stronger and more generalized identification with that person than when resource-control is distributed among many agents. Thus, in a mother-child household where the mother has primary and exclusive responsibility for the care and training of the child, we would expect stronger identification with her than in the nuclear family, where these functions are to some degree at least shared with the father, or in extended families, where the functions are even more widely distributed by virtue of aunts, uncles, and grandparents.

Cultures may also differentiate the types of resources which a given parent may mediate. If, for example, a mother has primary control of food and love, whereas the father has control of administering physical punishment, we would predict that the child will identify with both of them, but with respect to different resources. To over-simplify, he will take after his mother with respect to love and affection, and his father with respect to power and authority.

CONTINGENCY OF MEDIATION

A child will manifest adult-role behavior under circumstances similar to those which have elicited similar behavior in the important agents who have socialized him. Thus, if the withholding or deprivation of resources has been contingent upon his bad behavior, and the giving of them contingent upon his good behavior, when he is in control of resources he will tend to manipulate them in like manner with respect to his peers. Similarly, if he has been given resources when he has a special need for them, e.g., solace when he is hurt, comfort when he is frightened, we predict that he will respond in this way to his peers when they are hurt or frightened.

MATURE SOCIAL BEHAVIOR

It should not be supposed that when the child becomes adult he will perform exclusively adult roles as we have defined them. Adult life requires that he not only mediate resources for others, but also that he accept the mediation of others. He must not only give but also accept gifts, must not only withhold resources from others or deprive them of resources—when this is the appropriate and responsible thing to do—but also must comply with others who appropriately deny resources to him. Sociability requires both nurturance and dependency, and to be effective in the complex structure of adult social life one must be able both to command and to obey. In other words, the adult role is to some degree a carryover of a part of the childhood role.

THE SUPEREGO

Our final derivation from this theory of resource-mediation relates to the development of the superego. We have suggested above that one of the contingencies of resource-mediation most likely to lead to learning by identification is that involved in the training of the child, that is, when resources are given when the child is good, withheld when he is naughty. Presuming that these circumstances will lead to a high degree of status-envy and frequent covert practice, we will assume that he will learn these disciplinary and "moral" roles of his parents.

Having learned these adult disciplinary roles, he will tend to respond to the "naughty" behavior of others as his parents have. Thus he will scold his siblings and playmates, even his parents, for wrongdoing. Young children have often been observed acting out parental behavior in their play with dolls.

Insofar as this acting out of parental disciplinary roles is successful with respect to others, he will tend to respond to his own wrongdoing with self-reproach and to his "good" behavior with self-praise. This may be derived from the principle of generalization which can be expressed in an oversimplified manner by the following formulation: "If I wish to be a parent I must punish naughty children. I am a child; therefore I must punish myself if I am naughty." In this view, then, the tendency to evaluate one's own responses derives from the process of identification with parents in the manner described above.

Our theory predicts another way by which the mediation of resources may lead to conformity to the cultural rules. As we have pointed out above, a child in interaction with his parents will have cognizance of their roles. Thus, he will be able to predict when they will punish him and when they will reward him. He may therefore conform, not from identification with his parents, but from his clear, and perhaps overgeneralized, cognizance of their disciplinary roles. In other words, a person may resist temptation for two quite different reasons: first, his anticipation of self-punishment derived from his identification with the parents' role, or, second, his anticipation of parental punishment derived from his cognizance of their disciplinary action. We presume that herein lies the difference between what has often been referred to as guilt and shame.

Bibliography

1. Maccoby, E. E. "Role-Taking in Childhood and Its Consequences for Social Learning," *Child Development*, XXX (June, 1959), 239–52.
2. Sears, R. R., E. E. Maccoby, and H. Levin. *Patterns of Child Rearing*. Evanston: Row, Peterson, & Company, 1957.
3. Whiting, J. W. M., and I. L. Child. *Child Training and Personality*. New Haven: Yale University Press, 1953.
4. Whiting, J. W. M., R. Kluckholn, and A. Anthony. "The Function of Male Initiation Ceremonies at Puberty," *Readings in Social Psychology*, edited by E. E. Maccoby, T. Newcomb, and E. Hartley. New York: Henry Holt & Company, Inc., 1958.

Personality Development
as Role-Learning

ORVILLE G. BRIM, JR.

IT IS OUR contention that the traditional approaches to personality which either assume, or seek to find and measure, "general characteristics," "source traits," "genotypes," "life styles," "basic factors," and the rest have taken the wrong road to understanding the person, and are in error in their fundamental premise that there are such general styles, characteristics, or traits. In contrast to this is a general theory of personality development, presented here in outline, which draws heavily on sociological concepts.

This theory sets forth the view that personality differences consist of interindividual differences in characteristics as expressed in social roles, and of little else. It holds that the proper explanatory variables include not only motivation, but also knowledge of the role demands and ability to perform. It maintains that variations in individual motivation, knowledge, and ability are produced not merely by cultural or idiosyncratic differences in background, but in addition by the types of social structure in which one has participated—the latter regulating, so to speak, which aspects of the culture one will learn.

A few observations are in order to clear the way. First, socialization is defined as a process of learning through which an individual is prepared, with varying degrees of success, to meet the requirements laid down by other members of society for his behavior in a variety of situations. These requirements are always attached to one or another of the recognized positions or statuses in this society such as husband, son, employee, and adult male. The behavior required of a person in a given position or status is considered to be his prescribed role, and the requirements themselves can be called role-prescriptions. In addition, the individual holding a given position has prescriptions concerning how people in other positions should behave toward him, as well as an understanding of what the others expect of him. Thus, between individuals in two social positions there are sets of reciprocal requirements or prescriptions, regulating the individuals' behavior towards each other.

If socialization is role-learning, it follows that socialization occurs throughout an individual's life. The new student, the army recruit, the young honeymooners—all become socialized as they enter their new statuses. It is fair to say that during the past decade probably the bulk of sociological research on socialization has not dealt with the process during childhood, but rather with entrance into roles during the adult period of life (2, 16). This work is often unrecognized by the persons engaged in it, or by students of personality development, as being systematically related to the study of socialization during childhood.

In any event, the concern in this essay is with personality development in children. That is, after all, the fundamental process. The socialization occurring during childhood correctly receives primary emphasis in research and theory. The potency and durability of the learning that occurs during this period is assumed on the basis of the frequency of learning situations, their primacy in the career of the organism, and the intensity of the rewards and punishments administered. Also, as McClelland (13) has argued, there is difficulty in extinguishing behavior learned in childhood because it was learned under conditions of partial reinforcement.

What is presented here builds upon the theories of personality presented by James (11), by the symbolic interactionists of an earlier day such as Cooley (6) and Mead (22), and by the latter-day protagonists of role-theories of personality such as Cottrell (7), Parsons (19; 20, Chap. 2), and Sullivan (17). However, in spite of the illustrious names associated with this approach to personality, at present it has yet to be explored in detail; Hall and Lindzey's (10) omission of a sociological theory of personality from their recent review volume, on the grounds that none was sufficiently developed, appears as a justified decision. This approach has never been pursued sufficiently to see whether or not, when one gets down to the level of data, it really leads to anything different from that being considered by traditional theories. Nor have the implications of this approach for traditional theories of personality been traced in sufficient detail to clarify the points of difference, and to make apparent its contribution of new concepts and principles.

No detailed exploration of this approach can be made in this essay. Instead, there is a quick journey down the main road to see where it leads. To anticipate what follows: through an expansion of some earlier ideas and by the judicious addition of some concepts, this approach to personality development does in fact lead to new things. For one, it points to research operations on some classes of variables that up to now have been related to personality development only in

unorganized ways. In addition, the general theoretical position advanced here seems to have the possibility of integrating
some of the different interests of sociologists and psychologists in personality.

Perhaps a word more needs to be said about the latter.
Much of the sociological interest in personality focuses on the
problem of how one's personality is related to deviance and
conformity in role performance, this being a central problem
in the analysis of social systems. The clinical and social-psy-
chological interest in personality has, of course, centered on
problems of content such as interindividual differences in
dominance, need for achievement, and the like. It now seems
that these two problems present different aspects of the same
more general problem, that of predicting individual variation
from some standard.

An individual's personality can be described by terms referring to his motives, his ideas, his behavior, or the results of
his actions. It has been pointed out (1, pp. 211–15; 3) that
role-prescriptions themselves are composed of statements
about the motives, beliefs, behavior, and effects which one
must display in the role. It follows that conformity and deviance, reckoned as they are in terms of the role-prescription,
must refer to variations in motives, ideas, behavior, or results.

Not only do the descriptions of content in personality and
the descriptions of conformity and deviance share these same
theoretical types of descriptive terms, but they share the actual
terms themselves. Thus, one person may be described as being
high on need for achievement where personality content is
involved. He may be described as being too ambitious where
conformity or deviance is the focus; for certainly one can be
deviant in a role only with respect to some prescribed characteristic.

Hence, we should recognize that the prediction problem in
each approach is really the same, namely, the prediction of

variation from some given standard. In the study of content in personality, the standard by which individual variation is judged is usually the average for a sample of subjects of which the individual is one; or some other samples of subjects on whom a test has been standardized. In the study of conformity and deviance the standard may be the accepted prescription for the particular role in question; it may, in research, be the sociologist's conception of the functional prerequisites of the role. Consider the similarity between the study by traditional personality theorists of why certain individuals are "high in dominance," and the study by sociologists of why certain individuals are "too dominant" (deviant) in roles prescribing comparatively submissive behavior. Since at a general level the problems are the same, it follows that there should be a set of concepts and principles that are suitable for the analysis both of content and of deviance in the study of personality.

It is one of the values of this approach to personality that it promises to supply just such concepts and principles. Indeed, the similarity between problems of the traditional personality theorists and those of the sociologists interested in social systems becomes visible only when the point of interest is the expression of personality within a role context.

THE DEPENDENT VARIABLES

With these beginning observations complete, let us turn directly to the task of presenting the analysis of personality development as role-learning. The first step is to indicate the kinds of dependent variables with which the theory is concerned. These dependent variables involve differences between individuals in some characteristics, whether of motives, ideas, behavior, or effects of their actions. In this, traditional personality theory and the approach to personality through role-learning are identical. The critical difference, however, between the two is in the level of specificity at which such personality characteristics are to be studied.

Traditional personality theories deal with personal characteristics at a most general level; the analysis of the situation in which high or low amounts of a given trait will be displayed has received some theoretical attention, of course, but the empirical work has dealt with the effects of electric shock, of simulated hostility in experimental small-group settings, and others, none of which remotely approach the degree of influence of the many different social-stimulus situations.

A next most specific level would be the specification of these traits within a role context, e.g., the person who is a dominant husband but a submissive storekeeper. A still more specific level follows from the fact that the behavior prescribed for a role may vary, depending on the person with whom one interacts. For example, the role of the salesgirl is quite different depending on whether she is interacting with her customer or with her floor manager. Gross and his colleagues have introduced the concept of role sector (9) to refer to the specific aspects of a role which pertain to interaction with other given persons, and Merton the concept of role set (15) to refer to those persons with whom the actor is concerned. However, even this does not lead us to the lowest important level of specification of personality traits. It may be that while behavior in a role is prescribed vis-à-vis specific others that there also are prescriptions regulating episodes within the ongoing interaction between persons. For example, are there not situations where it is expected by both the husband and the wife that he be angry towards her, and other occasions where it is expected that he be dependent, dominant, and so on?

One can argue that the "general trait" level, the "life style" approach to personality, has been unproductive; that it must necessarily be so; and that the study of personality must be more situationally specific. Whether an analysis in terms of roles, or even role sectors, is specific enough remains to be seen; i.e., research will indicate whether the gain in our predictive power is enough to warrant not moving down to an "episode" level. In any event, it is not necessary to take a position on the latter point in this essay, since the concepts advanced for the study of personality development involve learning in any normatively regulated social situation, whether roles or episodes.

What are some of the inadequacies of the traditional theories which conceive of the adult personality in terms of general characteristics? The common practice in these theories has been to conceptualize the personality in terms of settings on some of these traits; e.g., one is high, medium, or low on some of the many possible characteristics. Thus an individual may be introverted or extroverted; he may be anal-compulsive or not; he may be high or low in dependency, in aggression, in dominance, in nurturance and the rest. The more complicated theories include not one, but several, important traits and work toward the classification of adult personalities in terms of combinations of scores, or profiles, on this set of basic traits.

These general personality traits are viewed as abstractions from the individual's characteristic response pattern. Presumably they are discovered by studying the individual's behavior in all the important situations that he might meet, or by asking the individual to give verbal reports of his probable behavior in this sample of situations, and then striking an average. This approach leads to the idea of a consistent core of the personality, composed of a number of characteristics (e.g., "high dominance") with almost invariant settings. Research on personality development then looks at the socialization process to discover the antecedents of high or low scores for individuals on these various general traits.

This traditional approach, this search for general traits in the adult personality, can be viewed as a romantic quest which intrigues one by the possibility of discovering major life styles in individuals, but one which cannot succeed because an individual is not the same in different aspects of his life. It is confronted with the same troubles which plague the efforts to formulate the single master ethical principle applicable to behavior in all conceivable situations, namely, that moral rules differ from one situation to the next; in contrast, the successful religions of the world have great numbers of moral rules (and often not consistent ones) to cover all situations.

The utility of such theories depends on the degree to which they are able to predict the individual's behavior in many different situations, i.e., to predict the individual's behavior pattern in general, and this clearly depends on an individual's making about the same responses in all social situations. Few studies of the generality of characteristics have been made (13). Those which exist have dealt with linguistic, perceptual, motor, and other traits, and not with characteristics such as aggression or ascendancy. Even these studies do not sample from very different situations, and still the correlations are not high. Nevertheless, traditional personality theorists have gone ahead as if personality characteristics were in fact general; and studies proceed apace to identify the antecedents of these, without first ascertaining whether they really do have generality.

What would be found if the necessary research was carried out? Consider for a moment the case in which one has data consisting of correlations between measures of some trait made under different stimulus conditions; that is, in different social situations. Consider that these correlations may be respectably high, for example, around .60. There are two ways in which this consistency may arise. One develops when the actual values of the sets of scores are similar. Here one might speak of a consistency that is insensitive to changes in stimulus conditions.

A second way in which such correlations might arise develops when the ranks of the two or more sets of scores are similar. Here the scores might increase under one condition and decrease under another, but the amount of increase or decrease is similar for all subjects. Thus, the correlation between these scores under differing conditions could be high. One can speak here of a consistency of rank across situations. In one sense the trait is consistent in that one is able to predict the rank order of the subject, even though not the absolute value of his score.

Research may show that there are important personality characteristics which do have these kinds of generality. However, the available evidence is not promising in this respect. More likely is the following kind of situation. Consider the case where one has data of the same type (i.e., correlations between measures of a trait in different situations) but where the correlations are low, say around .20. Here the common practice in research on personality has been to deny the validity of the assessment procedure, and to redouble the effort to devise a new test, instead of considering the possibility that there is no general characteristic at all. For is it not true that the more likely explanation is that there is no consistency across situations, and that the effects of a situation differ depending on the personality characteristics of the subjects involved? Or, to put it in the same terms as our preceding remarks, the data would suggest that individuals behave in such a way that one cannot know, simply from knowing their expressions of a characteristic in some situation, either their actual score on a trait in another situation or their rank order with respect to other individuals in that same specific situation. If true, then this simple fact would account for the in-adequacies of traditional personality theories which are directed to discovering general traits.

Some will point out that there is in traditional personality theory another quite different conception of trait generality or consistency. It is the conception of the genotypic characteristic which may be expressed in diverse ways insofar as overt behavior is concerned, but which is present as an underlying and regulating trait in almost all situations. An individual may be basically (genotypically) hostile, for example, but the hostility may be expressed in many different ways in different social situations. It is, therefore, irrelevant to the issue of trait generality whether or not research finds similarities in overt performance; instead one must look for the underlying motives or attitudes, often unrecognized by the individual, which are constantly present under different disguises.

This conception of generality in personality characteristics is strongest in clinical theory. The fundamental defect of the conception is that it has neither been proved or disproved, and perhaps it never can be. The postulation of an underlying motive which explains a variety of overt acts is, in clinical work, *post hoc*. The assumed general trait serves as a heuristic device which guides the clinical inquiry; however in the absence of comparative studies, we do not know if it serves as well as would some other conception of personality. In any event, accepted studies which first assume the existence of such a genotypic trait in a sample of individuals, then stipulate what the evidence of its existence (and absence) will be in a variety of situations, then actually gather the data to validate the conception are not at hand. The genotypic conception of personality, if one were to take a harsh view, appears as a bit of legerdemain in which the theorist snatches identity from diversity by distracting one's attention from what one actually sees to something the theorist says is there, whether one can see it or not.

The actual lack of success of this traditional approach, entirely apart from other theoretical considerations to be advanced later, suggests the value of exploring a role-learning approach to personality development. This latter theory would view personality as composed of learned roles and role components, rather than of general traits descriptive of behavior across situations. It would be heartening to be able to refer to a large body of research, rather than the few studies (e.g., 8) that we have, showing how the characteristics of personality vary depending on the role one is in. But the work has not yet been done, and in lieu of it one must appeal to one's own familiar observations.

When one looks at what is actually going on around him, he finds striking the great variation in the individual's behavior from one situation to another during the course of the day: as the individual moves, for example, from his occupational role, to his various family roles, to his roles with the neighbors in the community, and so on. Recall the familiar example of the German adult male who is meek and subservient to his superiors in his occupational role, but who changes into a domineering, hostile, and aggressive father upon returning to his home. Consider the modern executive, who in his occupational role is autonomous, creative, and decisive but who upon going home and taking up his status as husband may become docile and dependent in family matters. What should capture the interest of the student of personality, therefore, is not the consistency of individual differences as he looks upon behavior. Rather it is the great adaptability, the truly impressive variation in response to situational demands, which characterizes man as he moves from one situation to another. The question becomes not "What is his life style?"

but instead, "How can it be that his character is continually transformed to accord with the social demands of his life?"

The case could hardly be otherwise; obviously roles demand quite different responses from individuals at different times. The not-so-obvious conclusion that follows is that the function of the socialization process is not to produce for society something such as the "dominant" individual or "dependent" person; socialization instead is aimed at producing individuals equipped to meet the variety of demands placed upon them by life in a society. Socialization is successful to the extent that it prepares individuals to perform adequately the many roles that will be expected of them in the normal course of their careers throughout society. It does this by increasing a person's repertoire of behavior; extending the range and increasing the complexity of responses which he has at his command; freeing him from a limited series of stereotyped responses; providing him with a richer set of discriminations between various social situations; and proliferating the specific motives which can be switched into action by appropriate social stimuli.

Especially one sees that socialization must develop the individual's potential responses along the whole range of variation of some given characteristic; for example, given the fact that different social situations require varying degrees of dominance, from high dominance in one to extreme submission in another, it follows that the successfully socialized individual must have acquired the ability to make responses with all different degrees of dominance. Nor is this true alone of dominance. This applies to all dimensional characteristics of behavior, whether they be achievement, nurturance, hostility, or whatever. Here, also, socialization to be successful must equip the individual to respond, when appropriate, with any given amount of a characteristic. One has to know how to get ahead in life, as well as how to relax. One has to know how to be kind to people, and how to be demanding of them. One has to know how to get angry, as well as how to be friendly.

The fact that research is able to find any consistency at all in individual responses across situations reflects several things. First, it may be taken as an indication of the fact that the socialization process is not completely successful. Consistency in the behavior of some individuals in varied social situations probably reflects the degree to which their socialization was unsuccessful and left them unable to meet the contrasting role demands. Perhaps one has not had experience in dealing with certain kinds of interaction situations and therefore generalizes from his limited repertoire of roles. Or, he may have had little training in discriminating between different roles, so that he appears socially crude and clumsy in his behavior by treating everybody alike. Thus traditional personality theory might be viewed as studying the waste materials, so to speak, of the socialization process, rather than the standard product itself.

Consistency may indicate only that the situations in which it is found have similar prescriptions for the individual's behavior. The consistency comes not from some unyielding trait of the individual, but from just the opposite source, his ability to meet the similar demands of similar social situations.

Some traits may show more consistency than others. These would tend to be functionally unimportant characteristics, their greater consistency arising because the expression of these characteristics is less regulated by situational norms. This reduced regulation in turn arises because these traits are less important to the success of the interaction.

Finally, some individuals may show consistency in some characteristics but not in others. Here a straightforward process of generalization of response from one highly salient role to others would seem to be the explanation. For example, the business executive whose major rewards are derived from his occupational role, and the bulk of whose time is spent in this social situation, may find the responses acquired in this role to remain relatively high in his response hierarchy, and continually to spill over, as it were, in response to the stimulus conditions of other roles; e.g., he begins to treat his wife as if she were his secretary and needs to be reminded of the fact that he is no longer at the office.

We come then, finally, to our dependent variables in the theory. These dependent variables are interindividual differences in characteristics as expressed within situational contexts; the central problem becomes one of predicting such situationally specific individual differences.

The choice of social situations for research attention is a matter of one's scientific interests, of opportunity, and of personal predilection. One might focus on the behavior of individuals in certain occupational roles, in their marital roles, in their roles as parents, in their relations to others in their neighborhoods, and so on.

The selection of the descriptive dimensions to be used in comparing individual performances in such situations must again be a matter of personal interest, current demand, and the like. Thus, one may be especially interested in differences between women, in the marital roles, in the amount of their dependency upon their husbands; or in the differences between physicians in the amounts of nurturance shown to their patients, as they fulfill their role as a doctor.

As we have noted before, the terms used to describe variations in behavior within these role contexts are the same terms as are employed traditionally to describe "general" characteristics of personality. Here though the application is made within specific social situations and not to life in general. The personality theorist especially interested in some given characteristic, such as dominance, now pursues his interest in this behavioral characteristic, but seeks to predict differences between individuals within roles, rather than across roles. Thus, the dependent variables of this theory are combinations of social contexts and selected descriptive terms: one is concerned with the unaggressive executive, the unresponsive wife, or the unaspiring student.

The limited development of the role-theory approach to personality is perhaps illustrated by the fact that there seem to be almost no concepts pertaining to these combinations of descriptive terms and social role. One example of this type of personality concept is found in the area of sex-role perform-ance, where the concept "homosexual" seems to refer both to a specific role and to a variation in behavior, i.e., the way a role is played. It is to be anticipated that as a role-approach develops, more concepts of this theoretical type can be formu-lated.

It is about this time that one might ask, "But what has be-come of the personality itself?" Many would say that to con-ceptualize the dependent variables in this way means that one is no longer studying personality, but only fragments of the individual's behavior that have little to do with his underlying character. The answer is that the learned repertoire of roles is the personality. There is nothing else. There is no "core" per-sonality underneath the behavior and feelings; there is no "central" monolithic self which lies beneath its various ex-ternal manifestations.

But, one says, what then of the self? The answer is that the "self" is a composite of many selves, each of them consisting of a set of self-perceptions which are specific to one or another major role, specific to the expectations of one or another sig-nificant reference group. The self-perceptions are of how one measures up to these expectations with respect to behaving adequately, possessing the right motives, producing the right results. The individual says, bringing together his many selves, "I am the person who is a husband, a father, a steam fitter, an Elk, a Democrat, and a Scout troop leader." The work by

Kuhn and his associates at Iowa (12) shows that when a person is asked, "Who are you?" he responds by saying, "I am a Catholic, I am a student, I am a man," and so on. Note that he does not respond by saying, "I am strong," "I am dominant," "I am dependent." When these responses do occur in the Iowa data it is almost without exception after production of the status names which mark the role conceptions of the self.

But, one says, the fact remains that one is conscious of one's self, that one looks inward upon something which he views as his true self, or looks outward upon an expression of his self in some particular context. This does not mean that there exists some separate, fundamental self. Rather, this is to be understood very simply as the individual bringing together, however briefly, the various categories of his self-perceptions in a full, composite image; or in the latter case, as the individual viewing and appraising his performance with respect to one reference group from the vantage point of another.

Where one does in fact view his "self" as co-extensive with one particular role, then there has occurred the elevation of one particular segment of the self to a dominant position. To some extent this occurs with all persons. There will be roles in which the rewards and punishments to the individual are much greater than in others, and which demand his continuing concern with their performance. Thus, for one individual most of his waking thoughts may be concerned with his performance and achievement in his occupational role; it is himself in this particular role which he tends to think of as his "real" self. This elliptical manner of speaking, however, is misleading and it would be wiser to speak of the one or two selves of most significance to the individual.

It follows, too, that evaluation of the self as being good or bad must proceed in terms of evaluations of one's behavior along certain dimensions within specific roles; one says, "I am a person who is a good husband," "a sometimes too cross father," "a successful business man," and the like. Self-evaluation means that the individual compares his own performance in the role with the expectations he perceives others to hold for him, or which he holds for himself because of earlier learning of what his parents or others would have expected.

One's self-evaluation can be realistic or not, depending primarily on two factors. The first is whether one's own evaluation of his role-performance is similar to that made by other people. Another is the correctness of his appraisal of others' expectations of him so that his evaluation of his role-performance is made according to valid standards. In the first instance, the concepts of role-model and of reference group refer to the events wherein the individual stops to ask himself how a given person—perhaps someone he admires—would carry out this particular role, and then seeks to emulate his performance. In the second instance he seeks to orient his role-performance towards the expectations he perceives some given group to hold.

Quite clearly there are many other points on which a comparison of traditional trait-theories and of role-theories would be instructive. One thinks of topics such as conformity; of how new situations are handled by the individual; of the questions of personality change and creativity; of how the concepts of the unconscious and the defenses are handled.

THE INTERVENING VARIABLES

The problem has been defined as the explanation of individual differences in behavior in specific social situations. What intervening variables will be useful in explaining such individual differences?

The intervening variables must pertain to what has been learned, for differences between persons arise in greatest part from differences in the content of prior experiences, that is, their socialization. Two questions thus arise: how one learns, and how this learning is to be described. Regarding the first, we need be concerned with detailed differences in learning theory. Many learning-theory issues are not pertinent to the level of inquiry of this kind of personality theory. It is necessary only to assume that the child learns from experience, and that the fundamental processes such as generalization and discrimination regulate this learning process.

The second appears as the critical question. The task of the intervening variables in this theory is to conceptualize what is learned. Here a role-theory of personality can make a contribution through its derivation from the more general analysis of conformity and deviance in role-performance.

The reference points for appraising the amount of individual variation are either the social norms (role-prescriptions) which regulate the social situation, or the median performance of persons in the role, which must reflect the social norms. Given this point of reference, then, in order to conform to such demands, an individual must know what is expected of him in a situation; he must have the ability to fulfill its demands upon him; and he must be motivated to do so. These three variables of awareness and knowledge of role demands, of ability to meet them, and of motivation to do so will serve in this theory as the intervening variables. They describe the learning that has accrued to the individual regarding a role. The major sources of variation between individuals in roles thus involve different degrees of ignorance of what is expected, different degrees of ability to learn and perform that which is expected, and different degrees of role-appropriate motivation.

This will be more familiar when one recognizes the contrast with traditional personality theory, where the major explanatory variable intervening between behavioral differences and prior learning has been that of motivation alone. There has been a pronounced tendency to view all learning as pertinent to the development of high or low strength of one or another motive, with the latter then carrying the burden of explanation of behavior variations. One possible contribution of a role-approach is to establish variations in ability to behave in certain ways, and in conceptions of what is expected in a situation, as intervening variables worthy of research.

Consider the examples of the unaggressive executive, the undemonstrative wife and the nonchalant student. To describe an individual's role-performance in these ways requires in each case some standard from which the performance departs. This may be the role-prescription by the employer, the husband, and the teacher, respectively; or the standard may be a more general consensus of how the role should be handled; or it may be the customary performance of a sample of other persons in the same role.

First, to a large extent an individual is aware of and conforms to others' expectations. Hence, where the individual varies from some prescribed standard the deviation may be because he is ignorant of this prescription, meanwhile endeavoring to conform to some other prescription that he perceives applies to the role. This causes him to differ from others in the same role, who are oriented to a set of prescriptions different from those he sees as applying to him. Thus, for our examples—the unaggressive executive, the undemonstrative wife, and the nonchalant student—the characteristics of their role-performance may stem from their ignorance of the prescriptions that their respective behavior be aggressive, demonstrative, and enterprising. One should note that their own particular responses to these social situations need not mean that other behavior is unavailable in their repertoire. On the contrary, the executive may demonstrate in other contexts that he knows full well how to be aggressive; the wife may be most affectionate with other people in other contexts; and the student may show tremendous enterprise in his peer-group athletics or in his adolescent business dealings. Nor need one conclude that these persons do not want to behave in the prescribed way. On the contrary, they wish desperately to be like other people in this situation but cannot because they are unaware of what they are supposed to do.

Second, the variations which occur in the performance of these three individuals may, in contrast to the above, arise instead from their inability to behave in the expected way, even though they know what this is and they wish to do it. One source of such inability is genetic. Another is acquired through physical handicap. Inability also results from failures in training for these roles. The aggressive behavior with respect to competitors expected of the executive may be a pattern of response which he failed to acquire or retain from his earlier experiences. The ability to demonstrate affection to her husband may well be something that the wife never acquired, possibly because of father absence and relative isolation from boys during her socialization period. The unproductive student may well know what level is required of him and may wish to reach this level but may not have the necessary intelligence.

Third, it may be that all three of these persons know what is expected of them and are able to conform to such demands, but that their difference from others in these situations is that they are unmotivated to behave in the expected ways. Differences in appropriate role motivation on the part of individuals indicate variation in, or in extreme cases failure of, earlier socialization. It is easily seen that variations between individuals in role-appropriate motivation may range from hostility towards and rejection of the role-performance through an affectively neutral position, to one of a high level of positive motivation in the role because of its considerable rewards for the individual. In like manner, the motives of a given individual vary between his many roles and may be substantially stronger in one role than another because of differential rewards. Thus, some individuals have a substantial preference for performance in their occupational in contrast to their familial roles, whereas for others the reverse is true.

These intervening variables could be employed in the classification of personalities. In existing theory the classification of personalities utilizes different settings on general traits. Here the classification, more specific to be sure, utilizes settings on such traits in given roles, and the relevant intervening variables. These items would define persons who are high or low on some given characteristic, in some given situation, because of ignorance, of inability, of inadequate motivation, or of some combination of these. Thus, an example is that class of women who rank low on the variable "demonstration of affection" in the situation called the role of the wife because the necessary responses are not part of their repertoire, that is, because of their inability to produce this behavior.

THE INDEPENDENT VARIABLES

We have stated that it is the differences in learning related to knowledge, ability, and motivation which underlie the situationally specific differences in personality. The next question, therefore, must be that of how such differences in learning occur.

Consider that in the society where a child matures there are always a great number of discriminably different social situations, each with its own norms, its specification of motives and behavior. We have argued that the acquisition of knowledge, ability, and motivation is always situationally specific. With respect to knowledge, as one observes the course of the child's day one is impressed by the time and effort directed to identifying and discriminating new situations; to gaining understanding of the precise combination of responses which is called for; to exploring the degree to which this new situation is similar to ones previously identified and from which prior behavior might be generalized. Regarding ability, one sees him trying new responses; seeking to develop his abilities to discharge successfully his role in some given situation; appraising his performance after the fact and discovering those parts of his behavior which require improvement. Last, although not observable directly, one views the child acquiring situationally appropriate motives; learning that it is a desirable thing for him to behave in way x in situation y, in other words, developing the motive to perform x in situation y.

There are two major types of variation, two fundamental classes of events, which one can discern in this vast and complicated socialization of the child. These two classes of events are the independent variables of the theory and serve to organize and describe systematically the sources of variation in learning that can accrue to children.

The first fundamental class of events pertains to the social-structural aspects of the child's environment, the network of related statuses in which he can be involved. The culture acquired by the child in socialization is associated with these specific interpersonal situations. The social structure through which he matures thus regulates in large degree which aspects of the culture the child will be exposed to and which he will learn. If certain statuses are not present in this social structure, it follows that the aspects of culture learned through interaction with individuals in such statuses are missed by the child, and that he remains deficient in learning in this respect, undeveloped in this potential aspect of his personality. Straightforward examples of these variations in social structure are the presence or absence of the father, the presence or absence of sibs of the same or opposite sex in the family, or the presence or absence of peers for the adolescent living upon the isolated farm. One can even conceive of differences in the overall "richness" of the social-structural environment of different children. Some children will grow up in a structure involving perhaps only one or both parents and themselves. Others will grow up in a crowded community with a large and extended family, where they are forced to differentiate between people in a complex social structure, and to acquire a wide response repertoire.

The importance of social-structure variation is based on several assumptions. One assumption is that what is learned in socialization is fairly large response units, involving inter-action episodes or even larger segments of role behavior. Social interaction is not made up of bits and pieces, of tiny unit responses such as a smile, a posture, and the like, put to-gether in a certain way upon this occasion. If this is attempted, role-performance becomes studied and false. Instead, it is something much more complex that is acquired all of a piece; consider the familiar example of the three-year-old suddenly playing the mother's role almost effortlessly.

A second assumption is that role-learning occurs from actual participation in interaction situations: the child must learn roles through interaction with individuals who are actu-ally in the various positions, or ones quite similar to the po-sitions, that he will encounter himself later on as an adult. This complicated learning process proceeds as the child moves from one experience to another during the course of the day, confronting in interaction a series of persons holding different statuses in the peer and adult world, who demand of him that he discriminate between them, that he behave in different ways towards them, and that he develop the desire to do so.

But these assumptions raise questions for which we have no answers. First, what of the implication that various roles or episodes cannot be learned vicariously, and cannot be taught by persons who are not actually in the position involved? One might say that this cannot be true: that always there is the ubiquitous parent, monitoring the child's actions as a representative of the larger society, overseeing and correcting behavior with respect to its appropriateness. The busy parent is concerned with the difficult tasks of teaching the child to be aggressive with his peer group, but not with his little sister; to be angry when he is insulted, but friendly when he is complimented; to be submissive to his adult superiors, but not necessarily so to his older siblings; to seek achievement in his school activities, but not in games with the family; to be dependent on his teacher in certain learning situations, but not upon his mother in other contexts. One sees that the function of these parental activities is to help the child to differentiate and understand the demands of the social structure. A parent's part in socialization often seems to be much more concerned with the child's behavior towards others than it is with the child's behavior toward the parent himself. Surely the child must learn something about interaction with others from listening to his parent's supervisory comments.

A second question is to what extent the parent can make up for the absence of important statuses in the social-structural environment of the child? At first it appears that the parent does little of this. Much of the parent's concern, described above, over the child's role behavior is directed to roles which the child actually has, rather than hypothetical roles which the child does not meet at all. Is not the parent's effort directed to teaching his son how to behave towards his younger brother, rather than teaching him how he should behave towards his sister, if in fact he had one? Although studies of the effects on children of the father's absence from the home have not had the same results, at least one (21) finds no large or durable effects. In this case the mother may be successful, either in acting the father's role or in training children in how they should act, if they had a father.

A third question is whether deficiencies in early life can be made up, so to speak, in adulthood through interaction with persons in statuses similar to those which were absent in earlier years. To what extent, or perhaps to what depth, is the socialization into adult roles, mentioned earlier, really successful? Does the person growing up without sisters and in relative isolation from age mates of the opposite sex readily overcome the effects of this deprivation of experience at a later time, for example, when he first gets into a co-educational environment at the college level? Or will he always be different because of this early deficiency of male-female peer interaction in his learning? Granted that certain people learn certain roles late in life, no one seems to know whether this is easier or harder, or simply makes no difference. A related matter is the use of role-playing as an educational and therapeutic procedure to overcome individual deficiencies in certain kinds of role-learning. The available evidence (14) leaves the question of its effects far from answered.

It is disappointing that there is an almost complete absence of research on the effects of social structure variation. There are a few studies on family size; a few on characteristics of siblings; a few on father absence; some impressionistic materials on the effects of grandparents, maids, and the like; but of the many thousands of research studies on child development there may be less than a hundred which relate variations in social structure to the developmental process and subsequent personality.

It may be that this research was not undertaken because it was hard to conceptualize the effects of social structure upon the personality. Or, it may be in part because this is viewed as lying within the sociological domain, and sociologists have only recently become active in number in the study of socialization. In any event, when variations in social structure are viewed as key circumstances which determine whether or not the child will be exposed to certain classes of learning, i.e., the learning related to certain kinds of roles, these variations can be dealt with systematically as experimental variables in studies of socialization. Out of this should come a better picture of the effects of the social structure on personality differences in later life.

The second fundamental class of events which regulates what is learned is the familiar one of cultural content. Because of its familiarity, only a brief review is warranted. We have stated above that the cultural content which the child learns in socialization is always attached to some specific interactional context, and that variations in the kinds of statuses he faces determine what is learned. Now, the second point is that the actual content associated with any particular role relationship—the characteristics of the interaction itself—will vary according to the particular culture or subculture in which it occurs. In different cultures, the conception of the desirable adult may differ and different ends may be sought in socialization. Or, there may be similarity in the values of different cultures, but disagreement on the means, i.e., on the ways children should be raised to produce the desired results. Thus in different cultures children interacting with some specific person in their social environment, for example, two boys interacting with their respective fathers, may be confronted with somewhat different experiences.

Another source of variation in the content of interaction is the expression of personal characteristics by the specific individuals actually occupying a given status with whom the child interacts. Every society allows individual variation in role-performance within certain prescribed limits. Thus there is always some amount of idiosyncratic difference in the experiences two boys will have in interacting with their fathers, even though the boys' cultural background is the same. The differences arise, of course, as each parent adapts his role (within the allowed range of variation) to better fit his own abilities and desires. The differences become then personality differences attributable to the parents' own socialization experiences.

This fundamental class of independent variables, namely, cultural and idiosyncratic differences in the actual nature of the interaction engaged in by the child, traditionally is studied under the concept of child-rearing practices. Studies of basic personality structure or of national character have sought to relate differences between cultures in certain content, for example, that of the mother-and-infant interaction system, to variations in subsequent personality. This same approach, of course, has been taken with subcultural groups where one studies the effects of the varying child-rearing practices of religious, ethnic, social-class and other groups. Last, studies of the effects of within-culture, but between-parent, variation probably constitute the bulk of existing work on personality development which relates child-rearing content to later personality. Familiar here are the many studies describing differences between parents in their role-performance, e.g., in the degree of rejection, the mode of discipline, the demand for independence, and the effects of such differences upon the child.

SOME IMPLICATIONS FOR RESEARCH AND THEORY

What activities do these new concepts suggest? We have stressed that the proper study of personality requires that one focus on interindividual differences within roles. We have said that the conception of intervening variables should include such things as one's understanding of what is expected in a situation. We have stated the importance of the social structure that is characteristic of a given child's environment, which channels and regulates the culture learned.

The concepts presented in this essay suggest some different approaches to familiar problems. For example, the appraisal of child-rearing practices (probably the major source of variation in personality in later life) should give more attention to the ways in which parents teach children to be aware of different roles. What of the differences between parents in how they actually perceive the social structure, and in the discriminations which they pass on to the child? Which areas of differentiation do they see as the most important? Which ones do they insist that the child learn? Conversely, which are those areas of social structure that a particular set of parents fails to emphasize? Consider common cultural distinctions such as those between male and female and the possible differences among parental couples in their emphasis upon these. Certainly there are parents for whom the male-female role differentiation is substantially less than for other couples. The same is true of the differentiation of power and authority between generations. Parents must differ markedly in the degree to which they insist the child distinguish between various age levels as statuses. These degrees of insistence must have significant effects upon the child's ability to discriminate different role situations and also upon his ability to understand what is expected of him, and should take their rightful place beside modes of discipline and other child-rearing variables.

As another instance, consider the situation where a wife is described as acting toward her husband as if he were her father; that is, she treats him as a father figure. Rather than consider this characteristic to be the expression of unconscious motives on her part, why not explore the alternative hypothesis which is that her behavior is the only kind of intimate, female-to-male interaction pattern that she knows? Then one looks for causes of this deficiency in her repertoire of action both in the content of the child-rearing experiences which she had and in the social-structural aspects of her early environment. Did she have the opportunity to interact, in a continuing and important relationship, with any man besides her father? Perhaps she never learned to discriminate between the different male-female status relations and never learned the behavior appropriate to each. A hypothesis is that wives who behave in this way come most frequently from families in which they were an only child; or, in any event, in which they had no brothers.

Something closely related to the preceding hypothesis is presented in an analysis (4) of a set of data originally collected by Helen Koch. These data consisted of teachers' ratings of children on many personality traits. All children had one sib. One finding was that boys with sisters had fewer masculine and more feminine traits than did boys with brothers. This was interpreted as the result of the necessary process of "taking the role of the other" in interaction, which in this case would lead to a dilution of the boy's own masculine responses. Now an additional and not incompatible interpretation is available with the concepts advanced here. Where the boy has only one sister, he learns peer level interaction patterns appropriate to a male-female relation. Certainly the expectations of his sister, and those of his parents for him toward her, include less aggression, less anger, and so on, than if another male (a brother) were involved. In the first-grade classroom he would tend, through generalization, to respond to his peers as he did to his sister, and hence would receive a lower rating on aggression and similar traits. As a firmer differentiation of male and female peers is learned, and the responses appropriate to interaction with both are acquired, these effects of sex of siblings should diminish.

What kind of research design is suggested by this view of

personality? An example would be a study which obtained data on a number of children describing their behavior (e.g., the amounts of aggression and dependency) in several roles, such as with their sibs, with their teachers, with their male and female nonfamily peers, and their parents. The study would consider as antecedents of role-specific differences between children such variables as their knowledge of the other person's prescriptions for them in the roles involved, their ability to make the appropriate responses, and their motivation to do so. This would lead, in turn, to obtaining data on the structural aspects of each child's environment (e.g., who are the people with whom he has an opportunity to interact?), and to an appraisal of the nature of the interaction.

One last point remains. It may appear that we have presented a theory with the dismal prospect of never being general; a theory that relates something like inability to be nurturant to one's wife to some specific experiences in childhood. What are the possibilities of becoming less specific by dealing with theoretical types of social-situational demands and with theoretical types of antecedents?

Suggestions of how one should classify situations include the ordering of situations in terms of their stimulus properties (e.g., in Murray's [18] conception of "press"), and the typing of situations in terms of the similarity of the behavior expressed in them (e.g., in Cattell's [5] work). So far these suggestions have not had any notable influence on the empirical study of personality. A quite different approach has been taken by certain sociologists, in which the basis of classification is similarity in the behavior that is normatively prescribed for the situations.

The leading example is in the work of Parsons (19), in which one finds the elements of social interaction set forth in terms of a few fundamental dichotomous variables, e.g., affectivity-affective neutrality. Parsons shows that the various theoretical elements descriptive of interaction can combine in different ways to delineate theoretically discrete and fundamental roles. As an example, he has described the role of the physician in our society as having a certain combination, or profile, of the theoretical elements. It is possible that there may be a number of other roles which are identical, at a theoretical level, with that of the physician. It then follows that there are some individuals who would differ from others in predictable ways in all roles of this type.

In a parallel manner, one looks for theoretical classes of independent events. These would not be the presence or absence of particular status occupants such as fathers, siblings, and the like, or the specific content related to these. Instead they would be the presence or absence of certain fundamental prototypical interaction experiences during childhood, whatever they may be, which serve as the material from which all roles are constructed.

In conclusion, this has been a long excursion through some difficult terrain and one can ask if it has all been worth while. Yet it is fair to say that the issues raised are real, that people do vary considerably in the way they perform different roles; that this is a matter of both scientific and practical concern; and that a major source of such variation must be the kinds of experience acquired in specific role contexts during the socialization process. Somehow these matters must enter more fully into our theories of personality development and into our future research.

Bibliography

1. Baldwin, A. L. *Behavior and Development in Childhood.*
   New York: The Dryden Press, 1955.
2. Becker, H. S., and J. W. Carper. "The Development of Identification with an Occupation," *American Journal of Sociology,* LXI (January, 1956), 289–98.
3. Brim, O. G., Jr. "The Parent-Child Relation as a Social System: I. Parent and Child Roles," *Child Development,*
   XXVIII (September, 1957), 343–64.
4. Brim, O. G., Jr. "Family Structure and Sex Role Learning by
   Children: A Further Analysis of Helen Koch's Data,"
   Sociometry, XXI (March, 1958), 1–16.
5. Cattell, R. B. *Personality and Motivation Structure and Measurement.* New York: World Book Co., 1957.
6. Cooley, C. H. *Human Nature and the Social Order.* New
   York: Charles Scribner's Sons, 1902.
7. Cottrell, L. S. "The Analysis of Situational Fields in Social
   Psychology," *American Sociological Review,* VII (June,
   1942), 105–17.
8. Goffman, E. *The Presentation of Self in Everyday Life.* Edinburgh: University of Edinburgh Social Science Research
   Center, 1956.
9. Gross, N. C., W. S. Mason, and A. W. McEachern. *Explorations in Role Analysis: Studies of the School Superintend-
   ency Role.* New York: John Wiley & Sons, Inc., 1958.
10. Hall, C. S., and G. Lindzey. *Theories of Personality.* New
    York: John Wiley & Sons, Inc., 1957.
11. James, W. *Psychology.* New York: Henry Holt and Co., 1904.
12. Kuhn, M. H., and T. S. McPartland. "An Empirical Investi-
    gation of Self-Attitudes," *American Sociological Review,*
    XIX (January, 1954), 68–76.

13. McClelland, D. *Personality*. New York: The Dryden Press, 1951.
14. Mann, J. H. "Experimental Evaluations of Role Playing." *Psychological Bulletin,* LIII (May, 1956), 53, 227–34.
15. Merton, R. K. "The Role Set: Problems of Sociological Theory," *British Journal of Sociology,* VIII (June, 1957), 106–20.
16. Merton, R. K., G. G. Reader, and P. L. Kendall (eds.). *The Student Physician: Introductory Series in the Sociology of Medical Education.* Cambridge: Harvard University Press, 1957.
17. Mullahy, P. (ed.). *The Contributions of Harry Stack Sullivan.* New York: Hermitage House, 1952.
18. Murray, H. A. *Explorations in Personality.* New York: Oxford University Press, 1938.
19. Parsons, T. *The Social System.* Glencoe: The Free Press, 1959. Chaps. 3, 6, 7.
20. Parsons, T. and R. F. Bales. *Family, Socialization and Interaction Process.* Glencoe: The Free Press, 1955.
21. Stolz, L. *Father Relations of War-Born Children.* Stanford: Stanford University Press, 1954.
22. Strauss, A. *The Social Psychology of George Herbert Mead.* Chicago: University of Chicago Press, 1956.

Index

The University of Texas Seventy-Fifth Year
Steering Committee

J. Alton Burdine

Samuel P. Ellison

William E. Keys

H. Y. McCown

Jack McGuire

H. H. Ransom

W. Gordon Whaley

John Arch White

L. D. Haskew, *Chairman*

W. D. Blunk, *Executive Director*

Committee for the Lecture Series on Personality
Development in Children

CHAIRMEN

Ira Iscoe, *Psychology*

Harold W. Stevenson, *Psychology*

MEMBERS

William Madsen, *Anthropology*

Clyde Martin, *Education*

Vere Devault, *Education*

Carson McGuire, *Educational Psychology*

Sallie Beth Moore, *Home Economics*

Phyllis Richards, *Home Economics*

Lora Lee Pederson, *Social Work*

Warner Gettys, *Sociology*